STEWARDSHIP:
Myth and Methods

STEWARDSHIP:
Myth and Methods

A Program Guide for Ministers and Lay Leaders

JOHN H. MacNAUGHTON

A Crossroad Book THE SEABURY PRESS · NEW YORK

The Seabury Press
815 Second Avenue
New York, N.Y. 10017

Copyright © 1975 by the Seabury Press, Inc.
Designed by Carol Basen
Printed in the United States of America

LIBRARY OF CONGRESS CATALOGING IN PERIODICAL DATA

MacNaughton, John H
  Stewardship—myth and methods.

  "A Crossroad book."
  1. Stewardship, Christian.   2. Church finance.
I. Title.
[BV772.M355]   248'.6   75–5878
ISBN 0–8164–2112–9

Contents

Introduction

In one of the Peanuts *cartoons, Sally, Charlie Brown's* friend, is pictured happily jumping rope. Suddenly, she stops, looks around, and bursts out crying. Charlie Brown enters the scene to ask, "What's the matter, Sally? What happened? Why are you crying?" To which Sally responds, "I don't know. I was jumping rope . . . everything was all right . . . when . . . I don't know . . . suddenly it all seemed so futile."

Perhaps "futile" is too strong a word to use about the feelings many church people harbor about the stewardship task in our parishes. Better words might be "frustrated," "uneasy," "confused," "apprehensive." Of all the things we do in the normal life of a parish church, few are approached with less educated enthusiasm and eager anticipation than is the annual spring or fall stewardship campaign. For many, the need of raising money in the Church is viewed much as the Victorians viewed sex. It is necessary but not nice. In the past decade, innumerable articles and books have been written trying to suggest that there is no essential cleavage between the sacred and the secular, between the material and the spiritual. In spite of that, however, there still seem to be multitudes of Christians, clergy and lay people alike, who see the fund-raising task in the parish church as an unwelcome interruption in the ongoing spiritual life of the parish.

At one extreme, the stewardship campaign is often treated clearly as an interruption, a little like a commercial message in the middle of a good television program. It is separated from the program itself in sound, content, and appearance with no connection with what went before and what will come after. It is kept as short as possible so we can, as quickly as possible, get on with the real spiritual thing we are here to do.

Or, at the other extreme, it is so unwelcome that it is soft-pedaled and wrapped in such a series of religious clichés and spiritual-sounding pieties as to go almost unnoticed.

There are obviously many exceptions, situations in which conscientious clergy and lay people are facing their fund-raising task for what it is—an opportunity for people to grow spiritually by a proper use and sharing of their possessions with God in God's world. But the feeling persists that these are the exceptions rather than the rule and that many of the faithful are still theologically and spiritually hung-up when stewardship time comes around.

The meaning of the very word *stewardship* has gone through a significant shift in the past thirty years. Not so many years ago, the word *stewardship* meant the annual subtle or not-so-subtle effort to separate parish members from their money in the support of the parish budget. More recently, perhaps because this definition seemed a little crass, the word began to take on a broader, more religious kind of definition. The United Stewardship Council, a little over thirty years ago, defined *stewardship* as "the practice of systematic and proportionate giving of time, abilities, and possessions, based upon the conviction that these are a trust from God, to be used in His service for the benefit of mankind." In 1950, the Joint Department of Stewardship and Benevolence of the National Council of Churches succeeded the United Stewardship Council, and this same definition was accepted by them with an amendment that added "in grateful acknowledgement of Christ's redeeming love" at the end.

I have no quarrel with the definition. I endorse it wholeheartedly. But even this was not the end of the evolution. In the past decade, and especially in the past five years, an even broader understanding of stewardship has emerged. Stewardship, and more specifically Christian stewardship, has come to mean: *"what we do with what we have all of the time."*

We have come to see, and quite correctly, that Christian stewardship involves every man in his relationship with God, involving the whole of man, relating in the whole of his life to his environment, to other people around him, and thus, fundamentally, to his God. Stewardship relates, we are learning, to how and in what ways we use everything God has given us. It includes our use of this created world and the space around it, life itself, our time, our skills, our relationships to people and things, and, incidentally, our use of our possessions. And therein, at least it seems to me, lie the seeds of a serious stewardship problem. This broader definition is very helpful and useful. But with it, perhaps subconsciously, the idea has also grown that it is somehow more spiritually worthy to talk about our stewardship of the earth (now called ecology) or our stewardship of relationships (now called interpersonal dynamics) than to talk plainly, and give it the same spiritual conviction and enthusiasm, of the stewardship of our material possessions, the stewardship of money. Indeed, some clergy will not speak of the latter at all, preferring to turn over the annual stewardship sermon (the money sermon, in plain language) to a layperson or a visiting speaker. Their preference, I suspect, stems only in small part from their real or imagined inability to speak on the subject. It seems rather to stem from the minister's belief that such a subject is just not quite proper for a minister in a Christian pulpit. When, out of necessity, ministers must address themselves to the subject, it is without much enthusiasm for the task.

Our stewardship campaigns themselves often betray the same misunderstanding. In one parish I served, the term *Every Member Canvass* was abandoned and changed to *Every Member Visitation*. While there was merit in the change, it was motivated primarily by a desire to change the campaign's image, so that the raising of money would take a backseat to a broader concern for the visiting of our membership. But, significantly, in actual practice the change was in image only, meant to soften the direct appeal for funds because a direct appeal for funds was deemed not quite worthy of the Christian Church.

Often we see campaigns broadened to seek pledges of time and talent in addition to pledges of money. Sometimes these are very well done and extremely helpful, both to parish families who can offer time and talent more easily than money and to the parish as an institution, which can use these gifts only too well. However, it can seriously be wondered if, in some cases, this combination kind of canvass is not, in fact, motivated by the underlying belief that adding the canvass for time and talent somehow makes the canvass for money in the Church more legitimate, a spiritual legitimacy which, in our minds, it doesn't quite seem to have in the Church on its own merit.

The purpose of this book is to suggest another way of looking at the stewardship task in parish life, based on several convictions.

1. The relationship of a person and his money is fundamentally a spiritual matter as fraught with implications and potential for an individual's spiritual life as is his

life of prayer or offering of time and talent to God in service to God's people. A writer of historical biography one time wrote:

Show me where a men spends his money and I will show you the real man.

Jesus, in the familiar words of Matt. 6 : 21, is quoted as saying:

Where your treasure is there shall your heart be also.

Both quotations suggest the same thing. Somehow, in some way, what a person does with his money, how he thinks about it, where he spends it, what he will do to earn it, and the things to which he will give it are some of the real clues to who he is inside, to what is essentially important to him, to what is really in his heart. It is significant to note the order of things in the words of Jesus. He does not say, "Where your heart is there shall your treasure be also." To be sure, the genuinely convicted Christian is very likely to express his conviction, his enthusiasm for Jesus Christ, in the way he thinks about and gives of his money. Really turned-on parishes, congregations with a genuine, enthusiastic commitment to Christ, seldom have financial problems. But what Jesus is saying in Matthew's Gospel is that it also works the other way around. Create the atmosphere in which a person can give of his treasure in a conscientious, committed, spiritually oriented manner, and his giving may become the channel through which his enthusiasm and commitment to Jesus Christ will grow and deepen and blossom into flower. If you doubt that, you could try an experiment. Go out and buy a few shares of stock in a legitimate business. Make it enough so your financial interest is important to you. Then notice what part of the newspaper you turn to first when you pick it up. I'd be willing to bet, three days out of four, it will be to the financial page to check on your investment. Interest and enthusiasm follow money. "Where your treasure is there shall your heart be also."

To put it another way, the places where we make our most serious financial investments, where we spend and/or conscientiously give of our money, are the places where our real self, our inner self as it really is, is going to be most interested, most teachable, most responsive, and most open. To deal with a person in terms of what he does with his money is to deal with most people where they really live. To effectively touch people in an area of their real interest and concern, as we can do in a properly conceived stewardship effort in the Church, can thus be to open for these same people an avenue to genuine spiritual growth, seldom open to us in any other way. Good stewardship has that potential. That, I believe, is something of what Jesus meant when he said, "Where your treasure is there shall your heart be also."

2. It is, therefore, extremely important that we build a proper and sound theological base for our stewardship efforts.

A *Peanuts* cartoon provides an illustration of what we are saying. Lucy and Linus are in the house looking out the window into a heavy rainstorm. Lucy says, "Boy, look at it rain. What if it floods the whole world?" To which Linus replies, "It will never do that. In the ninth chapter of Genesis God promised Noah that would never happen again, and the sign of the promise is the rainbow." Lucy is overcome and smiles out the window, saying, "You've taken a great load off my mind." To which, in the last frame, Linus replies, "Sound theology has a way of doing that."

The basic questions of life will, ultimately, be satisfied

only by theological answers. And this includes questions about money and our use of it.

A sound theology of money has a way of lifting the stewardship "load" off our minds, making it a joy rather than a burden. But, more important, it has the potential to tap the spiritual roots of Christians at a point where they are the most teachable because it is here where they are the most concerned. A well-conceived, theologically sound stewardship program can be the most exciting spiritual adventure you can undertake in parish life. If there is a primary thesis that runs through this book, this statement summarizes it as well as any.

3. A person, indeed a whole parish, can and should be enabled to grow spiritually in the life of grace and awareness of God through stewardship as well as in any other way.

It has been said: If you want to know about a man's religion, don't ask him how he feels about Jesus Christ, ask him how he feels about his property.

Much is said from the pulpit, in Bible study groups, and in informal conversations among church people about the concepts of God's grace, God's love, God's providence, all given freely to us. These concepts are among the most powerful themes in the Church. But more often than not, delivered in a religious context, these great ideas fall into a huge spiritual vacuum and are neither fully understood nor readily acted upon by church members.

A number of efforts have been made to measure the religious literacy of the typical Christian congregation. One such effort revealed the following. A simple sixth-grade test on Bible content was administered to an entering class of freshmen in a church-related college. Most of the students came from active Christian church families. Out of fifty questions on which sixth graders were supposed to score forty or above correct, the college freshmen averaged just under fourteen correct and the grades ranged as low as three out of fifty correct. Most didn't know what an Epistle was, none could name all twelve of the apostles, and only thirty-three out of the almost four hundred entering students could accurately describe what a parable was.

In another personal experiment I conducted in three different parishes, the results were similarly disappointing. Some years ago the National Council of Churches produced a multiple choice exam testing the knowledge of church people on the nature of God, the uniqueness of Jesus Christ, the nature of the Sacraments, and the nature and authority of the Bible, among other items. The multiple choices were a variety of separate denominational points of view on these issues with a sprinkling of non-Christian views. In my use of the instrument with vestries and Bible study groups in these three parishes, of the fifteen items included, the attempt to identify the Episcopal view resulted in an average of five correct, with answers ranging all the way from one out of fifteen correct up to fourteen out of fifteen correct. But the weight was clearly at the lower end of the spectrum.

And these test results are not untypical of the results of many other like testing experiments done in the Church. The fact is that, with precious few exceptions, the average church member who worships on Sunday morning in a typical church is religiously and spiritually illiterate and massively inarticulate. It should not surprise us, then, that when the profound concepts of the grace and love and providence of God are talked about in church, the response of most listeners is one of appropriate respect, because the words are familiar, but of little understanding and equally little appreciation and acceptance.

I don't want to overstate the case and suggest that a proper theology of money will suddenly make these great themes abundantly clear and understandable. I do want to say that it is possible that when we connect the ideas of God's love and providence and grace to something real in a person's experience, to something he lives with daily, the concepts are more likely to come alive for him, become understandable and even appealing to him, to the point where he is enabled to entertain them as true, begin to live with them, and even grow in grace with them. And what more real experience do most of us live with daily than our concern about and interest in our money? The struggle for financial security—a reasonable share of this world's goods, and all that implies of plain survival, status, comfort, and the ability to do some of the things we want to do—is a real part of every person's daily thoughts, aspirations, ambitions, and sometimes even his prayers. To enable a person to see this struggle as related to God's grace, God's providence, and God's love is, at least potentially, to enable him to see with new eyes what these powerful facts can mean in his life and, therefore, to enable him to grow in them toward God. The temptation to oversimplify and perhaps even overstate the point here is great. But experience demonstrates that it can and does happen.

What all this means in the daily round of stewardship is that the "why" and the "how" of our stewardship approach is as critical to the spiritual life of the parish and people in it as the number of dollars raised is critical to the financial and program support we need.

What follows is based on these fundamental convictions. It will be divided into three parts. The first will be an attempt to explore a biblical theology of money and its uses. The second part, in three chapters, will suggest some of the details of a well-conceived stewardship program. The third part is a collection of concrete materials that could be used or adapted in an actual stewardship campaign.

So if you are still with me, turn the page, and let's explore some theology together.

STEWARDSHIP:
Myth and Methods

chapter *1*

A foundation on which to build

When the stock market crashed in 1929, a lot of people found life a very heavy burden. Some jumped out of windows. Some lost their power to make decisions. Others did equally desperate things to themselves and others. Why? Because their god had died.

One day recently, I went shopping with my wife to buy a new winter coat. We were in the women's department of a large department store. While my wife shopped, I sat in the corner watching people as they browsed through the racks of clothes. One woman caught my eye, browsing as she was through the most expensive rack of pants suits in the store. She was well-dressed in the latest fashions and projected the image of a relatively affluent housewife. The clerk that waited on her was showing her almost everything that was there, without much success. And then, without any warning, the shopper dropped the last item on the floor and, in a rage, began to berate the clerk, the store, the manufacturer, and everyone else in sight about the outrageous prices, the gouging of customers by monthly interest rates on charge accounts, and the lousy fashion designers who changed styles constantly and forced her to change wardrobes with them to keep up. The rage lasted a full three to four minutes without any letup until finally she stomped away from the racks and was gone. I have never felt so sorry for a salesclerk as I did then. But why? Why the rage? My guess is that her god, money, had lost some of its power for her and was in danger of losing its control to comfort her.

These are both extreme examples to be sure. But they do illustrate the depth to which money—the getting of it, the spending of it, and the status and security it seems to promise—has always preoccupied people's minds. I believe this is increasingly true in our own generation.

Ask yourself this question. In the scale of things that are important to you, in what place would you put having enough money to do what you want to do? If you think deeply enough and consider it honestly, your answer will give you a pretty good indication of what you think about yourself and what you think about the kind of world in which you live. The value you give to having an adequate supply of money, or the ability to earn it, is probably the most accurate indication of the kind of satisfactions you want from life and what you believe it means to be fulfilled as a person.

Money, or the material things it will buy, has always held an important place in human society. Our possession of it, or lack of it, has always defined our ability to purchase goods and services. But for most of us, it also defines in significant measure the nature and limits of many of our personal relationships. Money is not only important for what it will buy, but for how it affects relationships between people, and relationships between people and their God.

I will never forget an experience I had in the early years of my ministry. It was in a small, struggling parish. In midsummer our water pipes sprang a leak. Nothing serious, but a steady leak outside the building. At our vestry meeting we had to decide what to do about it. Investigation had shown that the leak was on our property all right, but it came in the line at a place ahead of our water meter. It was on our property, and we were responsible for it, but it wasn't affecting our building, and it wasn't costing us anything. In the discussion, it was obvious that the decision was going to be to do nothing about it until the city discovered it and fixed it with city funds. Meekly, I suggested that there might be a moral issue involved, that we had a responsibility at least to report it (which might mean we'd have to fix it at church expense). The response I got was to be told nicely but firmly that I could have my morals, and they would have theirs. But right now we were talking about money. Then everyone laughed, and the meeting went on to other things.

Now these were not immoral men, calloused to moral considerations. But when it involved money, in this case just the Church's money, the cool blue of moral certainty became the faded gray of moral compromise. The men didn't change. The fact that their money was involved changed them. I was too young then to challenge them about it, and maybe I really didn't want to. And I thought no more about it. But I've never forgotten it.

We can add to that very simple experience a multitude of others where money has been a major factor, sometimes the controlling factor in human relationships. A thousand illustrations to suggest the point can be summed up in the often-quoted proverb, "Never borrow money from (or lend money to) a friend—or you will lose a friend." When money enters the picture, relationships change. Such is the power of money.

Ever since money evolved into a form in which it could be saved, the accumulation of money has been a genuine interest to most people and a consuming hunger in others.

For a great many people, primary elements of personality are subtly, or not so subtly, wrapped up in the green and silver ribbons of cold cash, or that which represents cold cash. Money is intimately connected with their sense of:

- Self-worth or lack of it

- Personal power or lack of it

- Status or lack of it

- Success or lack of it

- Internal satisfaction or lack of it

Whatever its economic purpose, money and the ability to earn it came to be regarded very early in human history as one of the clearest measures of the worth of human beings. Little has happened in history to suggest that this measure has lost any of its appeal or power over human life in our own time.

Many people are surprised to discover that Jesus understood, as well as any person who ever lived, this deep and compelling potential for good or ill in the relationship of a person and his money. If one were to ask a variety of people to name the subject Jesus talked about most, I suspect the answers would be forgiveness, prayer, sacrifice, joy, peace, the Kingdom of God. A careful reading of the New Testament, however, suggests another, and perhaps surprising, answer. The subject Jesus talked about most, as the New Testament records it, is the relationship of a person and his material possessions.

It has been established that fully one-sixth of all the words of Jesus in the New Testament are concerned with this one subject, and over one-third of all Jesus' parables are devoted to it. The fact is that the subject Jesus talked about more than any other was the proper use of one's possessions. To him, there was little else that could potentially deepen or destroy a person's relationship to God and to other human beings.

Consider only a few such obvious references in the Scriptures as the parable of the rich man and Lazarus (Luke 16:19–31), which relates vividly and unequivocally to the responsibilities and potential dangers of the misuse of wealth; the parable of the rich farmer (Luke 12:15–21), which relates to the temptations of greed; the teaching of Jesus on freedom from worry about possessions (Matt. 6:19–34), in the midst of the great collection of spiritual wisdom that is the Sermon on the Mount; and the story of the widow's mite (Mark 12:41–44), which relates to the spirit and motive of giving. And these are only a few of the many references that could be cited.

And Jesus was not alone in his concern. The Old Testament is heavy with references to the same subject. The prophet Amos speaks of how God's judgment will fall on those who selfishly earn and spend money and allow it to be valued ahead of their worship and before God (Amos 8:4–8). The writer of Deuteronomy, in a powerful passage that takes the form of a commandment, exhorts men to remember and thank God as the source of their wealth (Deut. 8:10–18). And throughout the Old Testament there are numerous references to tithing, not necessarily as a system for giving but as a way to be reminded that God is the source and giver of all wealth, to whom thanks is to be offered (Lev. 14:22, 27:30–33; Mal. 3:6–12).

In all of this, two things are clear. Money, and what it represents to us, has been a major preoccupation of every generation, as it is in ours. And Jesus, and others of God's men before him, understood that and tried to speak to the problem in many, many ways.

It is important for us, then, in trying to live in this world as religious people, to develop a clear understanding of the meaning of money—the theology of money, if you will. And as important as having a clearly thought out theology of money is making that theology evident to the people in the parish through the way in which we, as the Church, approach the stewardship task.

Yet, how badly some of us sometimes handle that task, year after year! There are as many different approaches to stewardship as there are parishes and years in which the task is undertaken. But the approaches I have observed nevertheless seem to break down into three major categories. I have to admit that I recognize these primarily because, at one time or another, I have used them all.

THE NUMBERS APPROACH

A parish sits down and calculates what it will need next year, in addition to what has been given this year, to carry out the Church's work in that parish. For example, let's suppose in a given parish, a 17 percent increase will be needed next year. And it's been carefully worked out: The church property is in disrepair and will need some work; the rector, a hard-working man, simply must be given a raise (and simply raising him to meet inflation won't do); the Sunday School program needs a lift for new materials and/or a paid director; a program we are trying to do in the community is in need of extra support; the diocese is asking us for more money for next year; and inflation has taken its toll on the Church budget as it has on the family budgets of its members. All told, we believe we can manage next year on about a 17 percent increase in our giving. So the message is communicated (either by implication or directly) that, therefore, if everyone would just raise their pledge for next year by 17 percent, we will make it fine. And thank you very much.

Perhaps that is overdrawn some, but in a thousand ways, this is the message that is delivered and heard. Now I'd like to suggest that there are several things wrong with that message.

1. IT PUTS THE EMPHASIS IN THE WRONG PLACE.

The Numbers Approach will always put the emphasis on the dollars the Church needs rather than on the giving. When you start with a budget, whether it be last year's (to which a percentage increase has been applied) or next year's (which incorporates that increase), the center of attention remains on the numbers, on the balance sheet. You can talk all you like about the programs or ministries that the numbers will pay for, or about giving as responsible Christians, but few will hear what you say because the natural tendency will be to sharpen their mental pencils to go over the Church's budgetary needs.

2. IT'S UNFAIR.

The basis of the message is that everyone is giving evenly, that parish family *A* and parish family *B* are already giving conscientiously in relation to their means and that a 17 percent increase from them both will continue to keep them conscientiously even. But the facts belie the assumption. While many families do give conscientiously, perhaps a great many more give, and will continue to give until challenged, far less than they could or should. To ask for a percentage increase, even by implication, puts an unfair burden on those who are doing their best to be faithful in their giving and allows the token giver to remain exactly where he is. Even if he responds to the percentage increase and gives it, he will, in all likelihood, remain what he has been, a token giver.

3. GENERALLY, THIS APPROACH REPRESENTS A MINIMUM RATHER THAN A MAXIMUM REQUEST.

It has been said that politics is the science of accomplishing what is reasonably possible. Politicians could take lessons from church vestries and finance committees. When the subject of next year's budget comes up, some important questions are either seldom asked or are given short consideration:

- What do we really need?

- What do we really want to do here?

- What things would we really like to do if money were not a problem?

They aren't asked because what occupies the mind is the single question:

- What can we reasonably expect to get?

Perhaps it is the fear of asking too much and facing failure that tempers us. Maybe it's just our reluctance to ask at all that frightens us. But with the Numbers Approach, what we ask as an increase is pretty well educated by what we are fairly certain is attainable, or by how far short of our goal we can reasonably fall without getting hurt. Thus, the asking is generally calculated to meet a minimum standard of giving dictated by timidity rather than any maximum effort dictated by creative imagination about ministry and opportunity.

4. IT DOESN'T CHALLENGE ANYONE SPIRITUALLY.

One of the deepest concerns about much of the church fund raising we see is that we ask our people to give to the Church, or to a given parish, when what we really need is to ask them to give to God. The effect of asking people to give to the Church is to base our appeal on the people's responsibility for the survival of the parish, on parish loyalties, on interest in parish activities, or even on loyalty to a particular parish priest. None of these are so much wrong or bad as they are incomplete. To base our appeal on these things is often to preclude any serious consideration of giving as a matter of a person's spiritual life, as a serious matter between a Christian and God.

We, who are church people, always operate on at least three levels in our spiritual life. We live on the level of denominational loyalty. That loyalty may be very strong or very weak, but one thing that holds us to the Church is our denominational bonds. In addition to that, we live on the level of parish loyalty. To work in a particular parish, to give to that parish, is to be tied into an interest in seeing that parish survive, prosper, and grow. However, our parish and denominational loyalties are sometimes unbending, locking us into an attitude that is offended when things change. To see what is happening in the Church today and to see the response of many church members to what's happening is to see this locked-in attitude with crystal clarity. Beyond these loyalties, we also live on the level of a loyalty—a commitment—to God in Jesus Christ. At our best, all three loyalties complement and reinforce each other. However, one cannot help but observe that, all too often, the first two loyalties are used as a substitute for the third. We are so easily caught up in a kind of "Churchianity" that shuts out the growth of our Christianity. Indeed, to be faithful to a church is a far easier commitment than to be faithful to Christ, or so it seems. And when we deal with our stewardship task on the level of either denominational or parish commitments, we run the real risk of allowing these to be a substitute for any challenge to grow in relationship and commitment to God. Again, while we may *say* that our stewardship is a matter of the spirit, a matter of a person and God, when the push really comes, it's the other necessities and other loyalties on which we are really banking. That's the real message church members will hear loud and clear and assume they are being asked to respond to.

THE "AREN'T YOU ASHAMED OF YOURSELF" APPROACH

Using this method, someone takes the trouble to find out where people are spending their money, and if it's done thoroughly, the information can be rather precise. The message comes across something like this.

Someone has recently done a study on where people spend their money. And this is what they discovered. Nationally, we spend roughly:

$3 billion on cosmetics and personal care . . .

$3 billion on tobacco . . .

$10 billion on recreation and entertainment . . .

$12 billion on alcoholic beverages (with their attendant headaches) . . .

$9 billion on jewelry, furs, gambling, and other luxuries . . .
(and here is the kicker)

$1.5 billion on churches and other charities of our choice.
What this means is that we care roughly:

$2\frac{1}{2}$ times as much about our personal care than we do about God . . .

$2\frac{1}{2}$ times more about our cigarettes than we do about the Church . . .

8 times more about entertaining ourselves and our children than we do about providing our children with a religious education . . .

10 times more about drinking than we do about praying . . .

7 times more about our luxuries than we do about the Church's necessities . . .

And the climax of all that is the finger-pointing question, stated or implied, "Aren't you ashamed of yourself?"

The approach is summed up neatly in a little poem I clipped out of a parish newsletter not so long ago. It was labeled "Quote of the Week" and was used during the stewardship drive.

> Four thousand for my brand new car,
>   Six thousand for a piece of sod,
> Twelve thousand I paid to begin a house,
>   A dollar I gave to God.
>
> A tidy sum to entertain
>   My friends in pointless chatter,
> And when this world goes crazy mad,
>   I ask, "Lord, what's the matter?"
>
> Yet there is one big question
>   For the answer I will search,
> With things so bad in this old world,
>   What's holding back my church?

Obviously, the great appeal of such an approach is that it is all too true. The priorities of most Americans are clear. From the point of view of religionists, they are somewhat, if not deeply, mixed up. The temptation to call that to the attention of the people and use that call as the base for additional giving is very great.

But there are some liabilities in this approach that beg to be pointed out.

1. IT APPEALS TO GUILT, OF WHICH PEOPLE HAVE
   TOO MUCH ALREADY, AND LAYS A HEAVIER
   BURDEN OF GUILT UPON THEM.

If we are concerned in our stewardship solely with the raising of money, this approach might well satisfy our needs. Done right, it probably will shake a few extra dollars loose in the form of pledges from time to time. It will do so because we all know that the facts are correct. Our priorities are less admirable than they could be.

But if our intention in stewardship is to enable us to recognize the acts of God in our behalf and to make a deeper commitment to God through our giving, then guilt and adding to that burden of guilt surely do not make a useful base for such growth. To be sure, our feelings of guilt sometimes do bring us to a kind of repentance that will change our priorities. But far more often, it is the very sense of guilt that drives us away from God.

I've never run a scientific survey of the attitudes and feelings of church people, but my unscientific guess, based on twenty years of parish ministry, is that one of our most deep-seated and universal feelings is an uneasy sense of unworthiness before God. Most Christians sense that, somehow, because of our plain sinfulness, we must earn our way into God's favor. To be sure, there are many in our time who grandly and vigorously reject any idea of sinfulness on their part. These will proclaim loudly and often that sin is obsolete, especially their own, and that what they seek and will find is acceptance for what they are and are in the process of becoming. But their very bravado often betrays them. For underneath all these claims, I believe, many are not all that sure. Indeed, some are absolutely sure that they are not good enough, nor will they ever be. The burden of guilt they carry is the major source of their claims to be free of judgment. It is almost as though they desperately hope that if they shout "freedom from guilt" loud enough, it just might come true. But as I view church people, whether they claim the obsolescence of sin or not, this sense of unworthiness before God seems more and more evident.

John Snow, in a recent book titled *The Gospel in a Broken World*, makes the same point in a whole different context.

To say to the average American today that God loves him is probably to him the most preposterous statement that could be made. . . . After all, he smokes, drinks, possibly uses drugs, swears, increasingly goofs off at work, has been or is sexually promiscuous (at least by God's standards), . . . and on occasion spends more than he earns. He is, by traditional standards, an object for cosmic punishment and not for God's love (p. 41).

Of course, the Gospel that we proclaim insists that human beings *are* the objects of God's love. The love and salvation of God in Christ is freely offered and freely given. The Gospel does not demand that we meet some standard before we can be loved and accepted by God. But that is a terribly difficult message for most of us to hear and appropriate.

If, in the stewardship task, we deny that message and instead feed our sense of guilt and intensify it, what spiritual growth can there be? We may shake a few billfolds a little harder, but we also run the real risk of driving people away from the very God we proclaim and worship.

2. CRITICISM FOR FAILURE SELDOM STIMULATES PEOPLE TO DO THEIR BEST.

Giving, be it to the Church or to any worthy cause, is not an intellectual process but an emotional process. Most giving is done because a person has been motivated by his feelings, feelings stirred by truths that have been presented to him in a way that he can understand. To accuse people of not giving what they ought to give puts them on the defensive rather than motivating them to give more, responsibly. Child psychology has long ago recognized that behavior in a child is modified by approval and acceptance far more readily than by criticism. In the stewardship task we need to learn that same lesson. More will be said about this very big subject later.

THE "CRY POOR" APPROACH

Through both the written and spoken word, the message communicated by this approach comes out something like this.

Friends, we are living in perilous times. For some years now, our parish has been here on this corner serving and ministering to the needs of our people. But this year, we are in grave danger. After years of distinguished ministry we have come to the crossroads. One road leads to further ministry. The other to a severe cutback in ministry. To continue to serve, there are some things we simply must do.

And here are listed all the desperate needs, which might include leaks in the roof, cracks in the parking lot surface, malfunction in the heating equipment requiring major repair, the need for secretarial help, janitorial help, a whole new Sunday School curriculum, etc. The climax is reached as the appeal is made.

Unless we receive substantially increased pledges, we simply cannot do these necessary things for which we do not now have enough money.

It all adds up to a message that says, "Poor old St. ————. Won't you all please dig a little deeper to help her out in this time of crisis?" Sometimes this message is delivered when the crisis is real enough. Sometimes the message is delivered when there is no crisis, or at least no crisis as perilous as is described. The theory, of course, is that very few people can resist such a plea from their own parish and will indeed respond to save the parish from a fate worse than death.

Clearly, nothing is wrong with a special appeal based on legitimate need, when that need is laid upon us. But as a regular diet, this approach seems to have some severe liabilities.

1. IT APPEALS TO FAILURE INSTEAD OF
   EFFECTIVE SUCCESS.

If there is a single principle in modern advertising that runs through almost every ad, it is the principle that success begets success, failure begets failure. The proud claims of a great variety of businesses advertising today are all claims of success. One hamburger vendor claims that "10 billion have already been sold." Another claims having assets of X millions of dollars and "going up." Another claims to have so-and-so, the professional football (baseball, hockey) player as a customer. All this is done to present a picture of success that will attract new customers. The premise is that people want to be associated with successful things and will spend their money where success is already proven. To cry poor in business is the death knell. In the Church it may work once, but in the long run, this approach will lose you money, members, and enthusiasm.

2. IT TRIES TO MOTIVATE GIVING OUT OF PITY
INSTEAD OF THANKSGIVING.

I happen to believe in the Church and the God of the Church. I also believe in the actual worth and the tremendous potential worth of the parish church as a setting where the God-man and man-man spiritual encounters can take place and be fostered. The parish church, while it is sometimes ineffective and dull, will nonetheless never become effective and alive from pity. Indeed, pity for the old church is an unworthy motive to sustain any effective stewardship, or anything else for that matter.

ANOTHER APPROACH

Now, to be sure, some of what has been said above is overdrawn and stereotyped, but it ought to lead us to consider other ways of thinking about our stewardship. Experience shows that there is a way that is more theologically and biblically sound and much more spiritually challenging to church people than the approaches described above, a way that will also evoke greater participation and better feeling on the part of church people. Incidentally, it will produce a more adequate financial response as well. And it requires that we go back into Scripture for our background.

As noted earlier, the Bible is full of references to man and his relationship to material possessions. What are some of these references, and what do they have to say to us?

The book of Genesis begins with the words:

In the beginning God created the heavens and the earth.

The theme of God's ownership, through creating, and man's trusteeship (stewardship of the earth and what is in it), sounded here in the first verses of Genesis, is a recurring biblical theme in both the Old and the New Testaments. The writer of Deuteronomy (Deut. 8:10–18) picks up the theme. After listing many of the accomplishments of man's hand—his house, the building of his herds and flocks, and his accumulation of money—he then warns his readers that the temptation to consider those things as his own will be great.

Beware lest you say in your heart, "My power, and the might of my hand has given me this wealth."

And the Deuteronomic writer lays it out clearly (Deut. 8:18):

You shall remember the Lord your God, for it is he who gives you power to get wealth.

God is the source, and man is the recipient and user of God's gifts. The book of Chronicles strikes the same theme again. David, near the end of his reign, has proclaimed a day of offering for the Temple of God. The initial offerings to God are from David's own hand. And then the text goes on, at length, to describe how the head of every household in the land came forward and made their freewill offerings. The climax of the incident is reached when the offering is concluded, and David addresses this prayer to God.

But who am I, and what is my people, that we should be able thus to offer willingly? For all things come from thee, and of thy own have we given thee. . . . Lord our God, all this abundance that we have provided for building thee a house for thy holy name comes from thy hand and is all thy own. (1 Chron. 29:14–16)

Again, in a more indirect way, the same theme is caught by the prophet Malachi. In severe words of judgment, Malachi, speaking for God, chastises the people for withholding their offerings to God, calling it robbery.

Will man rob God? Yet you are robbing me. But you say, "How are we robbing thee?" In your tithes and offerings. . . . Bring the full tithe into the storehouse. (Mal. 3:8–10)

The assumption of the whole passage is that God is the owner of all things, and not to return to God of what he has given you, in this case a tithe, is robbery. The emphasis on the tithe here is less important, in my view, than the principle that provokes it, God's ownership of all things and man's trusteeship.

Turning to the New Testament, we hear the same basic principle sounded again. In three parables especially, Jesus uses this theme of God's ownership and man's trusteeship. In the parable of the talents (Matt. 25:14–30), one of the few parables appearing in all four Gospels, Jesus is saying that whatever we possess (it matters not whether we interpret talents to mean money, as in the parable, or skills, opportunities, creative talents, education, or even life itself), we possess because it has been given by God's hand. And from the gift, some return to God is expected. (And again it matters not whether we see the return in terms of a consecrated life, service to our fellow men, or offerings of money that God's gifts have produced.) The point of the parable is God's ownership and man's trusteeship.

Another parable puts it equally well, the parable of the tenants (Mark 12:1–12). In this parable, which has to do with the rejection of God's Son by the Jews, the underlying theme is the assumption that what man has, he has because it has been given to him at the hands of God. And from the gift, a return is expected.

And yet a third parable suggests a similar theme. The

parable of the laborers in the vineyard (Matt. 20:1–16) clearly describes the proposition that God is a giver of gifts and that God's gifts exceed anything we can do to earn them. The poignancy of the words of the parable, "Am I not allowed to do what I choose with what belongs to me," put in the mouth of God, is a proclamation of the depth out of which God desires to give of "what belongs to me" (note the emphasis on God's ownership) to his people.

Other references can be examined, but these suffice to suggest that a theology of money, a theology of what we possess, begins with the principle that what we have, we have been given. The source of these gifts is a God who loves us and wants the best for us.

Now let's try to be a little more precise about it. When we speak of God's ownership and man's trusteeship, how do we translate that from the Scripture to the world in which we live? There are many ways to illustrate this translation, but I have used three illustrations that make sense to me and seem to be understandable to others. The first comes from the world of agriculture.

Not so many years ago, the Associated Press released a study done by an agricultural school in Iowa. It reported that production of 100 bushels of corn from one acre of land, in addition to the many hours of the farmer's labor, required 4,000,000 pounds of water, 6,800 pounds of oxygen, 5,200 pounds of carbon, 160 pounds of nitrogen, 125 pounds of potassium, 75 pounds of yellow sulphur, and other elements too numerous to list. And in addition to these things, which no man can produce, rain and sunshine at the right time are critical. It was estimated, the report went on to say, that only 5 percent of the produce of a farm can be attributed to man's efforts.

Indeed, the earth is the Lord's, and we are the recipients of great gifts.

Another illustration of the same point, much more simply and directly made, is a homely four-line poem.

> Back of the loaf is the snowy flour,
> And back of the flour, the mill.
> And back of the mill are the wheat and the showers
> And the sun and the Father's will.

Indeed, "All things come of thee, O Lord."

A third illustration comes from a lawyer's office. Some years ago a Louisiana law firm was asked to undertake a title search for some property in New Orleans. They successfully traced the title back to the Louisiana Purchase in 1803. But their clients were not satisfied with that. So the search went on. Finally, the law firm sent the following letter to their clients.

Gentlemen:

Please be advised that in the year 1803, the United States of America acquired the territory of Louisiana from the Republic of France, by purchase. The Republic of France, in turn, acquired title from the Spanish Crown by conquest; the Spanish Crown having obtained it by virtue of the discoveries of one Christopher Columbus, who had been authorized to undertake his voyage by Isabella, Queen of Spain, who obtained sanction for the journey from the Pope, the Vicar of Christ, who is the Son and Heir of Almighty God, who made Louisiana.

What we are accustomed to call our own is not really ours. It is God's. What we do is to hold it for a time, use it, add to it, and then pass it on. God is the owner. We are the trustees.

Now these illustrations are fine—as far as they go. They are understandable, I believe, because the vast majority of thoughtful people, when it is called to their attention, really do believe that they have been given bountiful gifts of God's hand.

But it is not quite as simple as that. In modern America, where the Protestant work ethic has had such a hold on us, where competition and pride of accomplishment are so deeply built into our economic life, there are many who argue that what they have, they have by their own sweat and hard work. Some will argue the point with fierceness born out of genuine pride. For some, their pride of economic accomplishment is a very large part of their ego-support system. A good illustration of this is seen in the attitude of a great many hard-working people about the so-called welfare mother. The woman is often young and physically fit enough to work. But she stays home with her children and is supported by public assistance. It is said by some, and believed by many, many more, that these mothers should get about supporting themselves. "After all," they say, "no one is supporting me. I have to go out and earn it. And so should they." For some, the words are more refined than that. But what are they really saying? Behind these words is another meaning, having nothing to do with welfare mothers at all, but with themselves: "Look at me. Look at what I have done and at what I have by my own plain hard work." Of course, they are quite correct about what they have done. To say to them that what they have, they have because God has given it to them is to say something, at best, only half believed. So we must go on and say more.

Here is an illustration that helps to lead into the more we need to say.

A minister once went out to visit one of his parish members. He lived in a run-down house with a front yard that had been left in a real tangle of weeds and brush and tall grass. But within a few months after he bought the place the man had literally transformed that front yard into a beautiful lawn and garden. When the minister called, he saw the wondrous improvement. He said to the man, "My, isn't it wonderful what you and God have been able to do with this yard?" The man thought for a moment and then replied, "Yes, it is, but you should have seen it when God had it alone."

The story has value because it points to the obvious truth that much of what we have, we have because we have worked for it, because we have been willing to invest our time and effort and enthusiasm and money. It is out of a sharp awareness of their sweat and toil that many people claim pride of ownership, a pride of accomplishment, and so easily say, "Look at what I have done." There is no question that for a great many hard-working people, it is the simple truth, as far as it goes.

But biblical theology asks a man to take one more step. It asks him also to acknowledge that what he has done, he has done because he has been the recipient of countless gifts. A life to live, he didn't earn that. A brain with which to think, a talent to use, these things we have not earned. The raw materials of the earth with which to create, a body with which to work, and countless opportunities in which to grow, learn, mature, and develop as a person—these are not earned, these are given. While people may vary tremendously in what each one will make of these gifts, basically and undeniably, they are gifts given for which no man may claim responsibility. If this message can be communicated and heard, a man may then grow to the point of being able to say, "Look what I have done, with what God has given me." Indeed, one may even grow to the point of being able to say, "Isn't that something of what life is about, to take what we have been given—in ourselves, in other people, and in the earth—to use it, to develop it, and from it to produce something of value, something of beauty in this world?" That something may be a product, a service, a better person, or a deeper relationship. But this understanding is possible only when we acknowledge that God is the owner and we are the trustees.

It seems to me that any coherent theology of money—the earning, spending, and giving of it—must begin with this.

This principle is expanded for a Christian in one magnificent way. The greatest gift of God to us has been the gift of His Son, Jesus Christ, and, through him, the opportunity to live in the power of the Holy Spirit. Clearly, when we have thought about the gifts of the earth, life and the human qualities of body, brain, talents, and the like, and identified these as gifts of God, we have only scratched the surface. As Christians we must go on and speak of what Paul calls "the unspeakable riches of Christ" (Eph. 3:8). Each reader will want to develop his own Christology. That is not our purpose here. But no discussion of God's gifts can ever be complete without some reference to the great (and wholly undeserved) gifts of:

An avenue of prayer available in the name of Christ Jesus,
The possibility of forgiveness through the intercession of
    Christ Jesus,
The assurance of salvation through the merits of Christ
    Jesus,
A life after death through the resurrection of Christ Jesus,
And a power to have and live a life abundant through living,
    in Paul's phrase, "in Christ Jesus."

Beyond this direct bounty, we do have, as all people do, the possibility of the life of joy in the power of the Holy Spirit.

Without detailing these things—for you can interpret their meaning for yourself—the point I am trying to make here is that we are the recipients of almost limitless gifts, through which we have all of what we possess and tend to call our own.

Now, what has all this to do with our giving? It is my belief that all this sets the motive for giving, a motive which is at once biblically sound and fundamentally appealing. We give because that is one way we have of directly expressing our thanksgiving to God for these gifts. The purest of motives for giving is to give because we have been given to. Giving can be our thankful response to God, who has given to us.

It is critical to note what that kind of motive does to (or for) the giver. To ask him to give out of thanksgiving is to ask him to relate creatively with his God and not to a parish budget. It asks him to respond out of what he has, i.e., his income, rather than to the needs of the Church. This makes giving a matter of spiritual life rather than a matter of parish survival. It asks a person to be a Christian with his money and not just a fund raiser and/or a budget supporter.

So, all in all, what have we said? We have tried to make four points :

1. Money, the earning and the spending of it, has always been one of the major preoccupations of people in all ages, including our own.

2. Jesus, and the prophets before him, understood the implications of this better than we do and, over and over again, spoke of the potential spiritual good or ill that rises out of man's relationship to his money.

3. The message of both the Old and New Testaments about our money is the powerful but simple reminder that God is the owner and the bountiful giver of both our

material and spiritual wealth, and we are recipients of these great gifts.

4. And that, in the recognition and acceptance of this basic fact, people can understand and come into a relationship with this God of grace and providence and love through their giving, motivated by their thanksgiving for these overwhelming gifts at God's hands.

It seems, at least to me, that a foundation built in principles at least akin to these I have suggested is not only desirable but essential to any stewardship effort we may undertake, if our stewardship is to be more than simply an effort to raise money. Indeed, built on such a foundation, our considerations of stewardship can then open up the genuine possibilities of spiritual growth, both in the life of the individual Christian and in the life of the parish as a whole.

chapter 2

But what about program and budget?

*In the last chapter we tried to take a look at our theo-*logical biblical foundations. We tried to suggest that giving is really a matter between a person and God. God is the giver, and people give as one way they can respond to God out of thanksgiving for the gifts received at God's hands.

But how does all that relate to our need to support a parish program and budget? And, more practically, what does all that say to the manner in which programs and budgets can best be presented in a stewardship campaign?

Before we get to a specific look at that question, there are two clear implications in what we are saying that need to be examined and understood.

1. *If Christian stewardship, in our context, is anchored in the relationship of a person and his money, then Christian stewardship will relate to a person's income, how he earns it, how he spends it, and if and how he decides to return a portion of it to God who is the ultimate source of it.* It does not relate to the Church's program or budget needs. The focus of stewardship is how the use of our money affects our relationship to God. To base our stewardship approach on the Church's budget and program is to shift the focus so as to get in the way of that larger consideration.

Some years ago the stewardship committee of a parish I served was wrestling with our plans for the coming fall canvass. Most of the questions we were dealing with were questions of program and budget adjustments we were going to have to make. We seemed to be getting nowhere with all of that as we tried to incorporate these needs into a theme for our canvass. And finally, after two hours of frustration, I suggested we break for the night. And then I asked the committee to take home an assignment. "We seem to be hung-up on what the Church needs and how much we think we can raise," I ventured. "So, would you go home and, for the next meeting, write a brief answer to this question: 'Why should anyone give anything at all to the Church?'" The answers that came back the next week were all essentially the same—and a surprise to almost everyone on the committee. One report that summarizes much of what was written came from a businessman who works in a highly competitive field.

Why should anyone given anything at all to the Church? I can only speak for myself. But for myself the answer is that I have been fortunate, blessed in many aspects of life, including my business, and I want to share this fortune with others. I don't think I feel guilty about all this good fortune, but I have come to realize that by no means have I been completely responsible for it, materially or otherwise. If this is so, then is it really mine to do with as I please? No, not really. I feel responsible to the source of these blessings and want to do the "right thing" with them. And as time has gone by, I've come to feel less and less that these things are my own doing. And at the same time, I've begun more and more to realize where they did come from—God. And the "right thing" has come more and more to mean what I think God would want me to do with my blessings. And one of the important "right things" is giving or sharing them with others.

Note some things about this response. It makes no reference to program and budget and the obvious need we faced to support them. But it puts the emphasis in the right place, (1) on the need to return to God out of thanksgiving, and (2) on basic income as the most immediately tangible measure of God's blessings and as the focus out of which his giving had to come. But, significantly, neither of these ideas was seriously considered by the committee until questions of program and budget had been put aside.

2. *It follows, then, that the stewardship campaign needs to be conducted prior to the formation of the parish budget.* The stewardship question ought never to be "How much do we need," or even the better question, "What programs can I help support." The basic question needs to be, "What do I have out of which I can conscientiously return, as a Christian, to God." Our need is to give to God and not to a budget and to give to God through many channels, of which the Church is only one. But basically when we pledge to the Church, we are giving, and need to know we are giving, to God, and not to the Church.

Another man on the same stewardship committee, an accountant who works as a corporation business manager, put his finger on it.

I want to give Him something in return, even though I could never begin to repay Him for all these blessings. How can I *give* anything to God? I can't touch Him. I can't see Him. But I can give to help others become more aware of His love for them. I can do this by giving to my Church, by giving gladly, even happily, *because the gift is for Him,* who has given me so much.

To talk budget and program to these people and to try to invent slogans to make that budget and program come alive, as we had tried to do for one whole night, was to miss the whole center of their motive to give. The budget and program just got in the way of their *Christian response* in giving. I suspect that there are many others who, while they may not say it the same way, feel the same thing. Even those who are often preoccupied with budgets may be so, consciously or otherwise, as a way of avoiding any demanding considerations of a more Christian giving response.

So the appeal needs to be directed toward a person's income, not the parish's need. Parish budgets need to be considered only after the stewardship campaign is completed.

But those two preliminary comments still leave us with the question: How, then, do we present program needs at stewardship time? Perhaps the distinctions I'm about to make will seem like drawing a fine line. But I believe them to be the difference of day and night.

1. PRESENT PROGRAM NEEDS IN TERMS OF THE
   CHALLENGE AND OPPORTUNITY OF MINISTRY.

People are seldom motivated to give to the Church as a church. They tend to want to give money to the Church (and to other charities as well) in order that the Church may minister, that is, that the Gospel may be preached, the sick visited, the bereaved comforted, the children taught the story of Christ, the adults enabled to learn and grow—so that the ministry of the Church may be taken from the building into the neighborhood, the diocese, the nation, the world.

Such presentations of ministry should not be labeled with price tags. In fact, they probably will not follow the line-by-line budget items you will later construct. What they constitute really is a parade of people and facilities, paid professionals and volunteers alike, who are ministering to the needs of the world and the people in it, in the name of Jesus Christ. The story of that ministry is told by people who are given flesh and blood and not by a set of figures in a column.

In other words, a dry presentation of figures, even if the need is described in terms of things to be done, is basically devoid of any appeal to the imagination. But to describe the work, to describe the opportunities, to describe the ministry that goes on, without the encumbrance of dollar signs, will enable people to put clothes and shoes and hands on their giving, bringing immense enjoyment and satisfaction to the giver.

Many parishes have already moved in this direction by organizing their actual post-canvass budgets into "ministries." While there are many ways it can be done, here is one effective way budget items could be listed:

- "The Ministry of Our Hands," which contains salaries and benefits for paid people . . .

- "The Ministry of Our Feet," which contains money given to work outside the parish . . .

- "The Ministry of Our Minds," which contains all educational work . . .

- "The Ministry of Our Voices," which contains the music program . . .

- "The Ministry of Our Hearts," which contains items of parish and inter-parish social-fellowship life . . .

- "The Ministry of Our Arms," which contains administration . . .

- "The Ministry of Our Muscles," for the housekeeping, janitorial items . . .

These categories (and others are available) might be advantageously tied together with Paul's phrase in 1 Corinthians 12:27, "Now you [plural, meaning the gathered Corinthian Church] are the body of Christ and individually members of it." A parish is the Body of Christ, so why not a budget designed in terms of the ministries of our various parts? But whether this or some other way is devised, the point is that program presentations need to be made incarnate, if I can use that word, given flesh and populated with people who do things, both in and out of the parish. Just picture the difference in appeal between the following two budgets:

1. Salary $ _____
   Car allowance $ _____
   Pension $ _____
   Sunday school $ _____
   Property maintenance $ _____
   Etc. $ _____

2. To minister to the human $ _____
      needs of our
      congregation
      (includes costs of salaries,
      etc., of clergy)

   To minister to human need $ _____
      outside the parish
      (includes cost of all
      outreach, missionary
      programs)

   To keep God's house decently $ _____
      and in order (property
      maintenance, etc.)

To sing the praises of God (music program)	$ _____
To deepen knowledge and faith among us (education program)	$ _____

The first is dry, dull, and boring. The other has people in it doing things and is, in that sense, alive.

This is not to say that there is any magic in simply reorganizing the budget figures under a different set of titles, although I believe that's a good thing to do. What I'm trying to suggest is that Church programs, actual or potential, have life when they can be seen as ministry and not just in terms of dollars needed. In such a presentation, prior to an Every Member Canvass, the cost of the various ministries shouldn't be talked about. It is the task that can be fulfilled, the help that can be offered, the word that can be spoken, the contact that can be made that capture the enthusiasm of people. Financial support can be discussed later, when your pledging is done and budget preparation time has arrived.

2. DREAM SOME DREAMS WITH YOUR CONGREGATION.

So often in program presentations at canvass time, even well-done presentations, we concentrate on things we want to do next year. While they may be urgent, the missing element is the far-out dream we may have. "What are we moving toward five years from now?" "Where are we going or where could we go in this parish if we had the courage and the funds three years or five years or even ten years from now?" One parish rector based one of his stewardship sermons on the theme "If I Had a Million Dollars." It was based on an old television series called "The Millionaire," in which a million dollars was given to a series of people as a gift. Each program then dealt with how they reacted and used that sudden wealth. His sermon asked the question, "What would we do with one million dollars if we had it in this parish?" Then he began to dream of things and happenings and ministries that might open up for that parish. He didn't get any one-million-dollar gifts, but he did open up the minds and the imaginations of the people to see what their tight budget had never allowed them to see, the possibilities there might be for that parish in the years ahead. People want to know, and really get turned on when they do know, that someone is looking ahead down the road, dreaming of what *might* be. Most people want to be a part of a dream, if that dream will serve the needs of people and is reasonably possible of fulfillment. And surely, it is only as we dream a little that these dreams might become reality.

3. INCLUDE IN ANY PROGRAM PRESENTATION A FULL SHARE OF SPACE AND IMAGINATION TO PROGRAMS OUTSIDE THE PARISH.

Parochialism is an insidious disease in the Church. It is never more insidious than when it invades our stewardship efforts. As the individual giver shares of his income with God through the Church, so the Church shares of its income outside itself. But because it is so much less visible, the ministry that takes place outside the parish needs clothes to wear in people's minds perhaps more than that which goes on inside the parish. The fact that much of the so-called missionary giving of many parishes nowadays is through agencies and boards (and therefore relatively anonymous to the giver) makes the problem even more urgent. I do not wish to return to the days when outside program people and missionaries needed to appear before us to plead for support. But there is a great need to personalize and visualize the ministries being undertaken in God's name everywhere. To lose it or minimize it at stewardship time is to miss a whole exciting, appealing and, I believe, necessary dimension of ministry in our world.

And there is another dimension to this problem.

It is one of the hardest lessons we need to learn. To shut out or minimize giving to legitimate causes outside the parish has the effect of minimizing giving to parish programs as well, whereas to support work outside the parish has the effect of broadening the base of parish support.

George Lundy, of Marts and Lundy, Inc., a New York–based firm providing consulting services to charitable and nonprofit organizations, discusses this phenomenon in the introduction of a book titled *Successful Fund Raising Sermons.*

I can't understand the ministers of the official boards of our churches who take the position that they will not allow their members to be solicited for outside enterprises. I suspect that it is because many of them are fearful that money given to enterprises outside of the church is bound to decrease the amount the church would have available for its own work. How wrong they are! I suspect this is because they do not understand another aspect of giving. It is not only an emotional thing, but it becomes a habitual thing; repeated giving develops "giving habit tracks" . . . , which makes it easier to do again. Giving makes it easier to give again, and the people who have developed a habit of giving are those who are inclined to give additional sums and who get greater satisfaction out of it. The churches which recognize this fact and see to it that other causes outside the church itself, such as colleges, hospitals, missions, etc., are given the opportunity to present their needs to its members are always the churches that find their own finances easiest. If I were pastor of a church I would see to it that every year the members of my church were given an opportunity to participate in these enterprises . . . , knowing the result would be more funds for my own work than I could possibly hope to have otherwise (pp. 10, 11).

4. MAKE YOUR PROGRAM PRESENTATION VISUAL
   AS WELL AS VERBAL.

It's an old but true cliché: a picture is worth a thousand words. And good pictures are not that hard to come by. The ministry, in and out of the church, can be dramatized by simple posters, by collages using magazine pictures and other handy, inexpensive materials, by photographs of actual parish activity, by slides, and transparencies. Indeed, by a multitude of visual aids, the parish program can be given wings on which to fly into the imaginations of the people.

One parish priest recently told me that for a year someone had taken photograph slides of virtually every aspect of parish life, some posed, some candid. To these were added some slides of work outside the parish in which the parish had an interest. With a tape recorder for a voice and three screens, a synchronized multimedia presentation was prepared for use at stewardship time. The emphasis of the presentation was to say, "This is what we can do with the gifts you give to God through this parish." And the effect was to create a new excitement about ministry in that parish and a genuine enthusiasm for being a part of it. Incidentally, it also resulted in a 25 percent increase in giving.

You don't have to be an artist or an expert to do these kinds of things. A search of your congregation will probably turn up several people who have both the skills and the interest to get it done. And that's a kind of stewardship in itself.

5. POPULATE YOUR PRESENTATION OF MINISTRY
   WITH FAMILIAR PEOPLE AND PLACES.

Nothing will provoke interest and make ministry come alive as quickly as seeing pictures of familiar people engaged in it. Ideas and programs are brought right down to home for the viewer. Familiar places (the church building, local hospitals, rest homes, the diocesan headquarters, and the neighborhood into which your ministry reaches) have the same appealing impact.

Moreover, unfamiliar people and places also take on a reality they might not otherwise have when seen in the context of these familiar people and places. It is as though you are saying, "Our ministry reaches out to where we have never been in person, but these unfamiliar people are essentially the same as you and me." Then people and places which had seemed insubstantial and abstract become less romantic and more solid and believable.

6. BE HONEST ABOUT WHAT IS REALLY HAPPENING.

You are not selling something; you are teaching something about the life of the parish ministry. The task is not to overstate the wonderful things that are happening in order to coax more dollars from people; the task is to inspire interest in the value and variety of ministry, to provoke insight and commitment. There is value, therefore, in illustrating failure as well as success. To say "We tried this and it didn't work out . . . but we did try and will continue to try other things" delivers the message of the continual search for ways to minister, a search that bespeaks of life and vitality. Or to say "Here is something we would like to do, where we see a need, and we would like to see how we in this parish can help to meet it" is to say, again, that the ministry is vital and dynamic, on the growing edge of service to others. Say only what is honestly possible, or already happening. You will inspire trust and belief and will provoke a more thoughtful and deeper response.

All of this might well be summed up by quoting George Lundy again.

Speaking as a layman I would say to you as pastors: Do not hesitate to present to us all the causes of the Kingdom in such a way that we can feel that we are really having a part in carrying them on, and you will not be disappointed in the result. Present them to us graphically so that we may be able to visualize them; dramatize them so that we may more clearly understand the opportunity for service that they provide . . . and we will not fail you. (Ibid., p. 11)

chapter 3

The day your dollar became a christian

The Right Reverend Basil Guy, Bishop of Bedford, Church of England, in a booklet titled *Stewardship Facts*, published by the National Council of Churches (1963–64), describes stewardship:

It is, of course, most happily true that whenever we begin to tackle seriously any one part of the Christian life, all the rest of life begins to come into sharper focus. It has been—and we thank God for it—the experience of many places that a stewardship campaign quickens and deepens the whole of Church life in a parish. But that does not alter the fact that stewardship is not a gospel, but a discipline; and if we ever allow ourselves to forget the basic fact we get into serious difficulty.

After an attempt to describe our foundations in steward-ship and some of the ways that those foundations relate to the presentation of parish programs and budget, we turn now to face the issue of stewardship as a discipline. If giving is a matter of man's spiritual life, if it can potentially relate a man in some creative way with his God, then how can the specifics of that man's giving be considered seriously and practically? How can a person who wants to be conscientiously Christian in his giving response to God translate that motive into a figure on a pledge card? Is there a discipline that can put these things together?

The answer, in my view, and in the view of many others, is *the principle of proportionate giving.* Simply stated, that principle says two things:

1. that our level of giving needs to rise out of our level of income, that is, out of the most tangible measure of the blessings received at God's hands, and

2. that giving out of thanks for these blessings will involve sharing a carefully thought out *portion* of that income with others (proportionate giving) in our gifts to God through the church and other charities of our choice.

Much is said in the Old Testament, and by a good many Christian leaders today, about tithing as the highest form of proportionate giving. The 10 percent tithe, with Old Testament texts to back it up, has often been held up as the standard for Christian stewards. And, obviously, there are a great many advantages to endorsing such a standard.

1. It is a biblical, albeit exclusively an Old Testament, standard.

2. It is related, as all giving should be, to income, and not to a church's needs.

3. It has a "universality" about it, in that the concept is as old as the early Old Testament, has survived through the ages, and is proclaimed and heard in our day across denominational lines of all sorts.

4. It could produce an astronomical amount of money in gifts, if subscribed to by even a substantial minority of our church families.

However, in spite of these clearly tempting advantages, I

am frankly not all that attracted to it. Some reasons for my lack of enthusiasm are as follows:

1. It is a legalistic system setting an amount to give instead of proclaiming a principle under which each person can seriously consider his own response to God, in freedom.

2. It is an Old Testament concept, perhaps significantly, not picked up and repeated in the New Testament. There are thirty-nine separate references to "the tithe" or to "giving the tenth share" in the Old Testament. The New Testament contains only four references to either term. Of those, the three in the Gospels (Matt. 23:23; Luke 11:42, 18:12) all refer to the practice in a judgmental context. The one remaining reference is in Hebrews 7:4–9, where it is not recommended, but used only in reference to a discussion of the Old Testament Levitical priesthood. This does not suggest that tithing no longer has validity, but it does suggest that we may have moved beyond it.

3. Because the tithe is unpalatable to many people, the very principle of proportionate giving is not seriously considered—and "the baby gets thrown out with the bath." The majority are tempted to retreat, as an alternative, into the old patterns of giving without reference to their means.

4. The tithe pronounces a judgment, implied or stated, on those who do not, because they feel they cannot, attain to it. To be sure, there are those who feel it *should* pronounce a judgment on nonparticipants, but I find that a stance with which I have the greatest of difficulties.

The fact is that no stated percentage gift adequately expresses our stewardship before God. Indeed, the fundamental relationship of God and man is not that of a master to a steward. The New Testament clearly related God and man, not as a master and steward, but as Father and Son. In the Gospels God is not pictured so much as someone who entrusts his property to a steward but as someone who gives his love to a son. And this is not merely a play on words. Try, for example, to expand the word stewardship so that it may include the concept of our sonship. We would put it in this way: "You are God's steward but you must exercise your stewardship as a son." But that puts the cart before the horse. It gives priority in the Christian life to the steward's qualities of faithfulness, responsibility, and integrity. But reverse the relationship. Say instead, "You are God's son and you are called to exercise your sonship as a faithful steward." Here it is the qualities of the son that come to the fore, the qualities of thankfulness, love, joy, and intimate relationship. And from this second view, another truth steps out for us. It is not a portion of what we have that belongs to God and therefore must be returned—all of what we have is God's, is the Father's. And far from returning that portion which is God's because it is his due from faithful stewards, we are called upon to return all of what we are given. And we return all of it, some in service, some in prayer, some in the quality of our relationship, some in talent developed and used, some in a life consecrated to Him, and some in specific material gifts, gifts of money thankfully calculated out of that part of God's bounty to us.

To be sure, both sets of qualities, those of the steward and those of the son, are part of our Christian response to God. But it is in the qualities of our sonship that the concept of proportionate giving has its resting place. The connection between the two can be stated this way: As sons of God, we have the relationship that speaks to the "why" of our giving; as proportionate givers, we have the discipline that speaks to the "how" of our giving.

The system can be described very easily. Take your annual gross income and simply multiply it by the percentage (3, 5, 10, 15 percent) that you want to share with God in your material giving. Then, in the case of an annual gift to God through the Church, simply divide that amount by the frequency with which the gift will be made in one year (fifty-two if weekly, four if quarterly, etc.).

For church people who are already making a gift, it might be more useful to begin where they are. Take your annual gross income and divide it into your present annual giving out of that income. This will give you the percentage of your income that that gift really represents. Then determine what proportion of your income you would like to share, to return materially to God. Then multiply your gross income by that percentage, and so on. As you can see, this can, and should, be put in very specific terms in relation to a church pledge.

For example, if your annual gross income is $10,000 a year and you give $2 a week to God through your Church, then it is helpful to know that your gift represents 1 percent of your income.

Or, if your annual gross income is $15,000 a year and you give $5 a week to God through your Church, your gift represents 1.7 percent of your income.

Or, if your annual gross income is $25,000 a year and you give $500 a year to God through your Church, your gift represents 2 percent of your income.

The figures that would be most helpful to use would be, of course, those that most closely match the incomes of the people in your congregation. For purposes of easy clarity, it might even be helpful in your presentation of proportionate giving to produce a chart like the one below, with the income figures matching those of your members.

Now, note how this chart is constructed.

1. The matter is stated positively. The chart does not say "if you wish to become a proportionate giver." The

A Guide to Proportionate Giving

IF YOUR ANNUAL GROSS INCOME IS:	YOUR PROPORTIONATE WEEKLY GIFT WOULD BE:				
	3%	4%	5%	10%	12%
$ 8,000	$ 4.62	$ 6.15	$ 7.70	$15.40	$ 18.46
9,000					
10,000					
12,000					
15,000					
17,500					
20,000					
50,000	26.92	38.46	48.00	96.00	115.38

assumption is that what has been said about proportionate giving has been heard and will be acted upon.

2. The chart begins at 3 percent as the lowest figure. Seventy-five to ninety percent of your congregation are probably now giving below that amount. The chart sets their sights a little higher at the start to show them what is really possible for them.

3. It doesn't stop at 10 percent as though that is the optimum gift. It shatters any limits, low or high, thus speaking to the principle of giving without fetters.

4. The chart speaks of gifts as weekly amounts. Monthly, quarterly, and annual giving are perfectly acceptable, but for most people, weekly giving has the advantage of not being overwhelming. People can consider a more substantial return to God if they are not reacting emotionally to a large annual amount. This is not to manipulate people into giving more than they can afford. But it is to give them the freedom to stretch their responding muscles to see further

into what is really within their reach. And more than that, a weekly gift has an appropriateness that matches the concurrent weekly offering of worship in which they engage. However, since income is earned and paid in varying ways, flexibility is necessary.

5. The amounts represented by the proportionate gifts will seldom come out to even dollar amounts. That has the real value of moving away from the prison that puts gifts in round numbers without basing the giving on any systematic measure. But a weekly gift of an odd amount—$9.23, for example—will continually focus attention on the percentage and will be a constant affirmation of the person as a proportionate giver every time the check is written all year long.

However the principle of proportionate giving is presented, the major advantages remain the same:

1. It puts the emphasis where it belongs—on giving out of income.

2. It allows the giver to consider and compute his gift according to a solid principle without putting fetters on his freedom to determine how he will apply that principle in his personal response on a pledge card.

3. It keeps a person honest about his giving, honest about the real value of his gift in relation to what he has. The measure is not, as it tends to be, by pure dollar amounts, against what others with more can give (imagined negative affirmation) or against what others with less are able to give (imagined positive affirmation). The measure remains where it needs to be, yourself against yourself, what you give against what you have.

4. It allows every person who participates to stand on equal ground as givers. The giver with modest income who gives 3 percent of that income is able to be affirmed in his

giving along with the big giver who gives 3 percent of a much larger income. Their dollar amounts will vary considerably, but each is sharing equally with God through the Church out of what he has.

5. And most significantly, it provides for those who want to be conscientious in their stewardship response to God a way to respond that has been carefully considered to the best of their ability.

Perhaps a final word is in order in regard to the power of proportionate giving. It seems to me that power flows in two directions, to the giver and to the receiver. We have alluded before to the need of people to know and to feel that they are okay—okay with others and okay with God. Clearly, participating in proportionate giving will not provide the total affirmation that people need from either others or God. But it is deeply affirming to anyone to know that he has seriously and conscientiously faced a daily issue in his life—the issue of the way to use his money. Call it affirmation or satisfaction or fulfillment or whatever. It is there.

As recently as 1973, the *Lutheran Standard* did a survey of some church members who had become proportionate givers in the past few years. Some of the results were printed in a bimonthly newsletter.

I first felt good about giving about three years ago. The turning point, I think, was when I realized that Christ really loved. I understand that all we have is from God, that we should return a portion of that to Him. But those things never really made it with me. I relate better to things Christ had to teach us, the things about loving. As Paul said, ". . . the greatest of these is love." I feel now when I give, I'm about his business of loving and it's great! [An electrical engineer]

The difference is feeling good about giving instead of feeling obligated. My giving to other things (family, friends, other charities) has increased considerably. [A university extension dairy agent]

We have learned that there is joy and satisfaction in giving proportionately . . . we have never been in need of anything, and every decision on our part to give more has invariably resulted in more (and unexpected) blessing, both monetary and otherwise. Putting the Lord first with your pocketbook helps you in putting the Lord first in other areas of your life. [An owner of a construction company]

They say miracles don't happen today, but we have had them happen in our lives since we pledged proportionate giving. Logically, we cannot explain how there were dollars to pay bills after writing our check to the church; how, at just the right time, job security came our way. As far as we are concerned you cannot afford not to be a proportionate giver. [An optician]

The experience mainly was deeper faith, love, and relationship to the Lord. It is just a joy I cannot explain. [A milkman]
                                    (*S.A.L.T.*, vol. 4, March–April 1973)

These families were identified as from five widely scattered states, as having incomes ranging from $10,000 to $25,000 annually, and as giving from 6 to 11 percent of income to church and charities combined. And one cannot help but observe how little their comments connected their giving to parish loyalty or program, in which they were deeply involved, and how central to their feelings were things like faith, joy, loving, and their sense of the Lord in their lives. These are not isolated individuals carefully selected, but are representative of the experience of thousands who have seen the power of proportionate giving to affirm them as persons and to work in their own lives.

Quite clearly, the other direction in which the power of proportionate giving flows is toward the receiver of these gifts; in our context, the parish church. To receive even minimum proportionate pledges from all of its member families would be a financial boon beyond imagining in most parishes. Indeed, where it is significantly practiced, proportionate giving puts financial worries to rest.

Recently, I saw the results of a study done in the Episcopal Church. It was calculated that if every Episcopal family in the nation were suddenly to become destitute and all of us were to go on Social Security at the lowest family income level, and then, if all of us, at that income level, were to give a proportionate gift of 5 percent to God through the Church, the income of the Church for God's work would increase seven times over. That's the power of proportionate giving to multiply parish income!

But more than the obvious financial results of such giving, there is another equally powerful consequence. In situations where proportionate giving has really taken hold, and where normal parish financial problems have been virtually eliminated, people seldom hold an attitude of complacency in their parish prosperity. Indeed, the feeling in such places is rather one of urgency—urgency about ministry both at home and away. One might guess that the urgency surfaced in the vacuum created where discussions of parish money problems had once been. But I think not. The more likely possibility is that the urgency came from the givers who extended their own stewardship into the life of the parish and led the parish as a whole to become a more responsible steward in ministry. Whatever the explanation, there are few of us who would not delight in that kind of urgency as a replacement for the urgency we all too often feel to meet the budget and see that all the bills get paid. Such is the promise and the power of proportionate giving as a way to express our thanksgiving to God.

This matter might well be summed up by an incident reported to be the true experience of an employee of the Internal Revenue Service.

The other day I checked a queer return. Some guy with an income of $5,000 claimed he gave $624 to some church. Sure, he was within the 20 percent limit, but it looked a little suspicious to me. So I dropped in on the guy and asked about his return. "Have you a receipt from the church?" I asked, figuring that would make him squirm. "Sure," he said, and off he went to bring the receipts. Well, he had me. One look and I knew he was on the level. So I apologized for bothering him, explaining I had to check out deductions that seemed unusually high. Upon leaving, he invited me to attend church with him. "Thanks," but I belong to a church myself," I replied. As I rode home, I couldn't help thinking about the man's interest in and fondness for his church and his unembarrassed, open invitation to me. I wondered, a little enviously, where he got his enthusiasm. It wasn't until Sunday morning when I put my usual two dollars in the offering plate that it came to me.

chapter 4

And now down to the nitty-gritty

Having attempted to describe some of the foundation blocks on which we build, we come now to the very practical problems of planning and executing the actual stewardship campaign in a parish.

Three basic assumptions underlie the details of this chapter:

1. One of the keys to an effective campaign is disciplined and detailed planning. More messages are delivered during a stewardship campaign by nonverbal means than by the words we speak. A poorly planned and conducted program will loudly proclam: "It is not important!" "It is not worth your best!" "It should not command your support!" A carefully worked out plan of presentation is essential:

- To achieve the best results, spiritually and financially

- To develop credibility—to assure people that you know what you are doing and are convinced of the value of it

- To enable people to make a considered response to something attractive and compelling

2. In order to maximize the results, an Every Member Canvass program needs to run a minimum of four weeks and can profitably involve up to six weeks of the attention of a congregation. A one- or two-week effort will generally achieve a minimum result. The digesting of ideas and materials to be presented and the building of the spirit of enthusiasm and the desired level of parish involvement require time. The pot needs warming before it will boil. Four to six weeks seems best to allow the process to happen.

3. The support and intimate involvement of the rector is an essential element. What we are about is fundamentally a spiritual task with potential for parish and people alike. It is an opportunity for the spiritual leader of a congregation to have an impact on the lives of people where they really live in a way seldom available to him. Moreover, to say that what we are doing has spiritual substance for our members and then to conduct the canvass without major involvement from the rector is to deny, nonverbally, the very message of our words. To be sure, there are many lay people who have both the skills and the spiritual depth to do everything I am suggesting—and to do it well. But it is the rector whose intimate involvement creates the essential spiritual base and credibility that are needed.

On the basis of these three assumptions, let's turn now to the detail work.

In a *Peanuts* cartoon, Snoopy is pictured in a tree deep in his Walter Mitty–style imaginings. He says, "Here's the fierce mountain lion waiting for his victim." Then Linus enters and Snoopy eyes him as his intended victim. He leers at him, poises himself, and then, with a scream, "Augh," he pounces. But the leap to light on Linus's head is without effect. Linus doesn't even blink. Snoopy, crestfallen, simply rides his perch in Linus's hair, saying, "Somehow my attack seems to lack force."

It is at the point of attack that we now stand. How can we give it force to command the attention and provoke the response of the congregation?

The elements we need to put together include the following:

1. A clear understanding of our biblical theology about money and specific ways in which that understanding will be communicated
2. A detailed calendar of all events to be undertaken
3. A specific method by which canvassers are to be selected
4. A specific way of training canvassers
5. A specific way of assigning canvasser calls
6. A system detailing:
   a. the content and timing of preliminary mailings to the parish
   b. the content and timing of sermons, talks by lay people, parish meetings, etc., so as to steadily build up to the time of pledging
   c. a system and time for preliminary canvasser calls on parish members
   d. all deadlines to be met by canvassers
   e. clean-up dates
   f. plans for a victory Thanksgiving celebration at the completion
   g. plans for reporting results to the parish membership

What follows in this chapter are some ways in which these things can be accomplished. Everything suggested here is subject to revision and adaptation to fit a variety of situations.

Assuming your annual campaign will take place in the fall, the following calendar is recommended.

A STEWARDSHIP CALENDAR

PRELIMINARY STEPS

June 1: Select the stewardship chairperson/people.
Their tasks over the summer should include:
  a. Selecting the specific theme and emphasis for this year, in conjunction with the rector and/or the stewardship committee
  b. Becoming familiar with and committed to the theology, the particular mechanics of your campaign, and any specific stewardship problems peculiar to your parish
  c. Reviewing and selecting, or writing (which I recommend, where possible), the stewardship mailing pieces you will use
  d. Selecting the key canvassers (about 20 percent of what you will need), contacting them, and securing their agreement to serve as leaders
  e. Establishing the stewardship calendar for that year, listing all major events planned

September 1: With the advice of the rector, and using the 20 percent of your leaders as contact men, all canvassers are now selected and their agreement to serve secured.

AT THE SEPTEMBER VESTRY MEETING: A complete rundown of plans, theme, materials to be used, and the calendar of events is presented for approval and support. Even if the preliminary planners are all vestry members, such a presentation will have the effect of clarifying the plans and giving the leadership a deadline to work toward.

September 1: All stewardship materials are to be on hand: pamphlets, pledge cards, posters, etc.

MID-OCTOBER: Parish stewardship training sessions: depending on numbers and circumstances, one, two, or three identical sessions may be needed. It is strongly recommended that *all* canvassers be required to attend a training session. (See Addendum 2.)

When these preliminary steps have been taken, then you are ready to launch the canvass itself. The calendar below is one way it has been done effectively. It is based on a five-week canvass, involving three Sundays.

THE EVERY MEMBER CANVASS

Week One

Prior to this, the stewardship leaders have been meeting. Simple announcements of those meetings have alerted the congregation to what is coming.

1. In the first "official" week, the *first mailing* to the whole parish is sent announcing and outlining the details of the program. Such a mailing should include:

- Dates and places of all events

- How and when pledges can be made

- What the canvassers will do

- Titles and themes of sermons to be given

- An invitation to participate in events

- A request for parish-wide prayers for the canvass, with an example of a prayer that could be used

It should also feature a written statement of basic theology of money, done with some imagination. (See examples in Chapter 5.)

2. The first canvasser call on parish families should be made now. This first call does not ask for, nor should it accept, any pledges. In fact, pledge cards should not be made available to anyone, except in very special circumstances, until Pledge Sunday. This call asks for participation in the events of the weeks ahead. The first call has four primary aims:
   a. To introduce the canvasser to his or her families (this initial call can also be used to update parish records, gather needed parish information, etc.)
   b. To explain details of the program and clarify any confusion
   c. To invite participation in and offer transportation to events, including Sunday services
   d. To encourage feedback on parish programs
3. Initial canvasser calls can be made:
   a. Individually in homes, which is usually most effective
   b. In canvasser's home by his or her invitation—an evening coffee, dessert, party, etc. (an informal, social evening; a low-key invitation to participation)
   c. By telephone, the least effective method

Week Two

1. Second mailing
   a. Reminder of details as outlined in the first mailing
   b. More on theology—different tack, same message (see examples in Chapter 5)

2. First Canvass Sunday
   a. Sunday sermon based on the theology of money (see examples in Chapter 5)
   b. Prayers for canvass in church
   c. A short service for commissioning of canvassers as part of your regular worship (see example in Chapter 5)
3. Potential parish meeting for presentation of ministry
   a. Evening session with supper
   b. Coffee-hour session following morning services

Week Three

1. Third mailing
   a. Move from "why" to the question of "how" to consider measuring your gift. An article on proportionate giving as a way to consider pledge (see examples in Chapter 5)
   b. Reminder of when and how to pledge
2. Second canvasser call, by phone or postcard, thanking families for participating in stewardship events thus far and encouraging attendance at remaining events, including Pledge Sunday
3. Sunday sermon on "Mission of the Church"
   a. Potential themes
      • What is the purpose of Church?
      • What is the purpose of (Name of your parish) ?
      • "If We Had a Million Dollars"
      (None of these deal with program or budget but with our basic reason for being.)
   b. Continued prayers for canvass
4. Potential parish meeting for presentation of ministry (see Week Two)

Week Four

1. Fourth mailing
   a. Move from "how" to the question of "how much." Include an article reinforcing the principle of proportionate giving as a way to consider pledging, backed up by a chart detailing pledges based on income to which a percentage has been applied (See example and discussion in Chapter 3.)
   b. Details about when and how to pledge
2. Third canvasser call, by phone or postcard, thanking families for participation and encouraging attendance at remaining events, especially Pledge Sunday
3. Sunday sermon on "Giving"
   It should deal with giving as a spiritual matter, and deal with money and giving directly and clearly. Include something on proportionate giving as a method (See examples in Chapter 5.)
4. Pledge Sunday
   a. Pledging can be done in church, following the sermon, while sitting in the pews
   b. All Canvassers meet at church, after services, for dessert and coffee. Canvassers receive names of those of their assigned families who did not pledge in church—to be called on *that afternoon*. Cards returned to central recording station by 6:00 P.M.

Week Five

1. Clean up all remaining calls. Don't allow it to get strung out—lose momentum, lose enthusiasm, lose impact. Calls not completed should be turned over to a clean-up committee
2. Report results to date to the parish—important for parish interest and satisfaction

POST CANVASS

1. After the five weeks, get cleaned up as rapidly as possible
2. Report final results to the parish, a complete report to be given two weeks after Pledge Sunday with the final results
3. Celebrate completion on Sunday with thanksgiving and joy
4. *Now*—get at budget preparation

GENERAL COMMENTS

If the life of a Christian depends, in part, on his giving . . .
If the life of the parish depends, in part, on being able to support salaries, program, buildings, outreach . . .
Then . . . the E.M.C. is one of your most important functions . . .
And . . . it deserves your best shot.

SELECTION, CARE, AND FEEDING OF STEWARDS
   (Some suggestions)

If your stewardship campaign is one of the major events of your parish year, the results of which will largely determine the extent of your parish program, and if your stewardship campaign is fundamentally a *spiritual* adventure, then who does your stewardship calling and how they do it become significant items.

Every parish will vary in how they select and train their stewards, but the following suggestions may be helpful.

SELECTING STEWARDS

1. Use your most active people regardless of how busy they are. The effort deserves the best. This is no time

to select someone "to help them become more active in the parish."

2. Select the people who are most likely to be recognized by your parish membership as the real leaders of your parish life. Those already involved and committed to your parish life are the ones who will carry the most authenticity when they speak to others.

3. Select those who are already your most sacrificial givers. Experience and established commitment are the best motivators in talking with others.

4. Select those who are able to recognize the value of a time schedule and the meeting of deadlines. Serious procrastination on the part of stewards is a heavy weight.

5. Generally speaking, a ration of one steward to seven families is ideal. One to ten seems maximum.

6. Do not hesitate to use women as well as men as stewards.

ASSIGNING THE CALLS

Methods of assigning calls will vary considerably depending on the size and circumstances of a parish. While many methods will be effective, the point is that *some method* must be used—the matter must not be left to a grab bag.

1. In a parish that is widespread, assigning calls by geographical neighborhoods may be your best guide.

2. Where feasible, calls should be assigned by approximate income levels, upper-income people calling on upper-income people, modest-income people calling on modest-income people, etc. These match-ups help communication, expectations, and effectiveness.

3. Stewards should be given the freedom to trade in an assigned call where there may be a personal conflict

that would prevent a positive contact from being made.

4. Women may be assigned to any calls, but sometimes it is helpful to assign a woman of standing in the parish to call on parish women who live alone.

TRAINING OF THE STEWARDS

1. In order to insure clarity of purpose and a united effort, *everyone* who is asked to make calls should attend a training session. In many places this is considered important enough to make it a requirement. To emphasize the importance of the task and to build some sense of stewardship team spirit, it is strongly recommended as a requirement.

2. The training session can be accomplished in one to one and a half hours. Where there are many stewards, two or three identical training sessions can be offered at different times.

3. The training session should include:

   a. A discussion of the theology, preferably led by the rector. (An outline of the key elements in such a presentation follows.)

   b. A review of expectations. What exactly do you expect of stewards, what are the deadlines, and how will what the stewards do fit in with the rest of your program? A systematic review of your calendar will answer these questions. In this area, assume nothing and be detailed in outlining the stewards' tasks.

   c. Help in very practical terms about methods of approach, i.e., the initial contact, later contacts, what can you say if . . . [the Church is criticized, the rector is criticized, a particular program in the Church is criticized; the person wants to give you a check for his whole pledge now; the person wants the card mailed to him; the person claims not to be a member, etc.].

d. An explanation of the Stewards Commissioning Service, if you have one.

e. Time to handle the questions, anxieties, frustrations of stewards so they can be made as comfortable and confident in their task as possible.

4. Open and close your training session with your parish stewardship prayer.

AN OUTLINE OF A CHRISTIAN THEOLOGY OF STEWARDSHIP

I.

1. No one who lives can reasonably live without seeing life as a gift. We have done nothing to earn it. We simply have it.

2. For a religious man, the source of that basic gift and, indeed, the very earth in which our gift of life is lived out, is a Creator-God who made it and gave it to us.

3. For the Christian man, the greatest gift, as important as life itself, is the gift of Jesus Christ, through whose life, death, and resurrection we can know and experience the love of God, here and hereafter.

4. In addition to these very basic God-given gifts, we have also been given a brain to think with, a body to work with, the raw materials of the world to create with, and countless opportunities in which to grow, learn, mature, and develop as people. While individuals vary profoundly as to what each one makes out of these gifts, they remain gifts for which no man can claim responsibility.

5. Therefore, when we deal with stewardship, we are not dealing with ways to convince people to give of what they own, but with the one basic need we all have—to share of

what we have been given. Stewardship involves everything we do all of the time. It involves our sharing of time, talent, and treasure—the traditional stewardship triangle. But it also involves our sharing of love, friendship, and concern, a less traditional stewardship triangle, and our sharing of these things in all our relationships, both in and out of the Church.

6. The specific claim of the Church on our sharing stems from our claim that it is the Church which is the major source of our understanding of this Creator-God, of the uniqueness of His Son, Jesus Christ, and of the power of the Holy Spirit that brings life to our life. It is in the Church, uniquely, that we can gather with other Christians to worship this God, to receive the Word and Sacraments and to find fellowship and mutual support for living in concert with other Christians. Pledging to God through the Church doesn't pay for these things; it just allows them to continue to be, and to be available to all men.

II.

1. It is common human experience that there is a profound kind of satisfaction that comes to us when we share openly. We make a living by what we earn; we make a life by what we share.

2. Somehow, we know, without really needing to be told, that to share is more mature, qualitatively better, than not to share. There is a moral rightness about sharing, a moral wrongness about failing to share.

3. Somehow, as a built-in part of our human nature, we also know that it is essential to our happiness to be sharers. To share openly is to find a kind of well-being that those who do not share do not seem to have.

4. All these things are not necessarily true because the

Church says so but because they are part of the very fabric of our basic human experience.

III.

Stemming from these things, then, certain principles of an annual giving campaign emerge.

1. We need to give to God through many channels; the Church is only one. When we pledge to the Church we are giving to God, not to the Church.

2. We give to God through the Church out of thanksgiving for what we have been given, not in relation to the needs of the Church; thus, a giving campaign must be conducted *prior to* the formation of a parish budget.

3. If giving is an act of thanksgiving, then we need to consider giving not in relation to what we can spare after other things are cared for, but in relation to what we have been given; that is, in relation to our basic income.

A SERVICE FOR THE COMMISSIONING OF CANVASSERS

The canvassers will come forward into the chancel, at the appropriate time during the Sunday morning worship service. As the canvassers stand in the chancel, the stewardship chairperson will say:

REVEREND SIR: These members of our parish have been selected to be canvassers for the Church.

RECTOR: Stewardship is a part of the spiritual life of every Christian and every Christian congregation. You have been selected in our congregation to assist in the stewardship program of this parish. Do you accept this responsibility?

CANVASSERS: We do.

RECTOR: Are you ready to carry out your responsibilities faithfully and completely?

CANVASSERS: We are, with God's help.

RECTOR: Let us pray for these stewards and the stewardship program of this parish.

Almighty God, the source of all that we have and all that we can hope for, strengthen, we pray, the hands of these canvassers as they move among the members of this parish. Grant that they may be able to speak clearly and listen carefully as they call in your name. Help us all in this parish to respond openly to share ourselves and our substances truly as your disciples. And grant that we all may see the fruit of our labors in a parish ever growing stronger in your service, through Jesus Christ our Lord. Amen.

I commission you Stewards of God and Canvassers in Church. Go forth in the power of the Spirit.

CONGREGATION AND CANVASSERS: Thanks be to God.

Then the regular service shall continue.

ADDENDUM I

On the Qualities of a Canvass Chairperson

Who should be selected to be chairperson of your Every Member Canvass? What qualifications should he or she have? The list below represents one man's answer to those important questions.

1. A person who understands and is personally committed to the theology of money and its uses. Whether this person will be used as a speaker or not, his or her commitment will shine through and influence everyone with whom he or she works.

2. A person who is organized and able to live within the

demands of a calendar and to encourage others to do so as well. There are those who, by nature, seem to have little awareness of the "times and the seasons." And they are beautiful people. But in the midst of an organized effort involving many people and many deadlines, such a person is unable to lead and will himself be led only to frustration.

3. A person who is immediately recognized by the congregation as one of its accepted leaders. This acceptance, acquired through other activities, gives the campaign instant credibility as one of the important events in parish life.

4. A person who in his or her own family practices the discipline of proportionate giving. This is far more important, in my view, than that the leader be one of the largest contributors. Again, the commitment of the leadership will shine through everything that is done or said and be a positive influence on everyone with whom he or she works.

5. A person whose faith in Jesus Christ is apparent and growing. A committed Christian response is seldom offered where the leadership hasn't already made such a commitment. Example is always louder than words.

6. A person who is able to have a positive rapport with the rector. The need for a close working relationship between these two is obvious.

ADDENDUM II

Recruiting

I have suggested that the canvassers be required to attend a training session. If a person is either unable or unwilling to attend such a session, you are probably further ahead to thank him and suggest that he or she might be better able to participate another year. Such a stance, while it may appear a little arbitrary, does in fact deliver a solid message to your canvassers. It tells them that you believe in the importance of what you are doing enough to take the time and effort to plan such a session. It tells them that what you are inviting them to engage in is a community effort in which others are making similar commitments.

The same principles apply to all kinds of recruiting in the Church. So often in the Church, it seems to me, we go out asking for volunteers in ways that are not helpful. In looking for Sunday School teachers, organizational officers, committee members, and sometimes even vestry members, we approach it as though we expect people to say no. We tell people things like, "The job is not too difficult; it won't take much of your time or effort; nothing much will be demanded or required of you, so why not accept the job?" But what are we really saying to the volunteer? Are we not saying, "The task is easy; anyone could do it; neither you nor your skills are especially important; what we are really asking for is a warm, live body to fill an inconsequential space." But supposing we go to our volunteer people, having thought it through, and say to them, "We have a task that needs doing as well as we can get it done. I'm asking you to help because you are the kind of person and have the kind of skills that are needed. It may be difficult at times, it will require a specific commitment of time and effort from you, but it is a task worth doing and you are the person we feel is best qualified to take it on." In this case, what have you said to your volunteer? You have said, "You are a person of real worth with something to give; we have thought it through carefully and selected you instead of others; the task is important and not just busy work and it will challenge you to get it done and satisfy you when it is completed."

It seems to me that this approach affirms both the person

of the volunteer and the importance of the task. And, beyond that, it affirms the value of the life of the parish and its total ministry to its people.

ADDENDUM III

Suggestions about Canvassers Calls

The initial contact you make as stewards will be an important one. For most calls, it will be about the same time that the first mailing piece has been received from the Church. Your task on the initial call is to remind people of the details of the program, to invite them to attend church, and to get acquainted with "your families." Everyone's particular style of contact will be different, but the following suggestions might be helpful.

1. Use your own natural style. A "canned" approach will seem artificial to those you are calling on and uncomfortable for you.
2. Tackle your easiest calls first. By the time you get to the less familiar calls, you will be an old hand at it.
3. Think about the people on whom you are calling. Consider their interests, their level of involvement in the Church, and any special circumstances you know about.
4. Get to the point of your call as soon as possible. This is not a social call, although it must be neighborly. Do not leave your family in doubt about the reason for your call. They are expecting to hear from you and most will welcome your contact.
5. Do not get drawn into controversy. If persons want to criticize the Church, *do not argue or defend.* Listen

politely, draw out as much detail on the complaint as possible, and assure the family that it will be passed on to the right persons. Write down as much as you can right after the call so it can be passed on accurately.

6. Do not linger. When you are sure your message has been understood and any comments from your hosts have been heard, conclude the call pleasantly, expectantly, and expeditiously.

7. Thank them for their time and courtesy to you and reinforce your hope to see them in church this Sunday.

8. Pray before each call, asking God to help you be clear, warm, and pleasant in what you say and open to hear what is said to you.

WHAT DO YOU SAY IF . . .

1. *Someone is critical of the clergy, the parish program, or someone or something about your parish life.*
   Respond sympathetically and openly. Do not argue or defend. For example, "I wasn't aware of the problem. Could you tell me something more about it so I can pass it on to whoever is involved?"

2. *Someone wants you to take their pledge now.*
   Thank them for offering but remind them that, for now, what you are asking is their attendance in church and their prayers for the stewardship program. If they insist, tell them you have no pledge cards and invite them to church on Pledge Sunday when pledge cards will be available for the first time.

3. *Someone doesn't want any more calls but wants to be put down for "the same as last year."*
   We don't want to encroach on anyone's time, but you do not have any pledge cards and it would be most helpful if they could sign the card themselves in

church on Pledge Sunday. If that's not possible, you would be glad to call in their home on or after that day to receive their pledge.

4. *Someone asks how much the budget is going up or what the Church needs, etc.*

"The Church has a great many needs, to be sure, but we don't have a budget yet. Our real hope is that people will consider their pledge in relation to their income, their ability to share, instead of in relation to the budget. After our membership has pledged as they can, then we will develop a budget out of anticipated income." Remind them that this very thing is what will be discussed in the Epistle and on Sundays and invite their attention and attendance to both.

chapter 5

Resources and examples

All the material that follows has been used in actual parish stewardship campaigns organized, with variations, on the principles and time tables described in the foregoing chapters.

SECTION ONE

Copy for mailing pieces that could be used according to the schedule suggested in Chapter 4. They may be used separately in the order in which they appear. Or they could be combined and/or adapted for fewer or more extensive mailings.

Exhibit 1

Example of first mailing

To be used in Week One

FALL STEWARDSHIP PROGRAM BEGINS

The time has again arrived to begin thinking about our Fall Stewardship Program. Over twenty-five to thirty members of the parish, under the leadership of Charles Converse and Dick Champ, have been thinking and planning for the program over the course of the summer and early fall. Seventy parish members, who have been selected as stewards, have already attended training sessions in preparation for the program.

The program, an outgrowth of last year's effort, will include some additional things this year that may be new to our parish.

1. Prior to October 15, *every family* in the parish will be contacted and especially invited to attend the Church services on three consecutive Sundays—October 15, 22, and 29. The program will be conducted over these three weeks. Every family will have an opportunity to talk with one of these seventy parish leaders as the program begins.

2. During these weeks, written material—in the Epistle—will go out to every family on the subject of stewardship, to suggest both a philosophy of Christian stewardship and the mechanics of our program.

3. On these three Sundays the Rector will be preaching three sermons around the stewardship theme. The sermon titles will be:

October 15 "Having, then, Gifts"
October 22 "If I Had a Million Dollars"
October 29 "The Subject Jesus Talked about Most"

4. On Sunday, October 29, parish families will be invited to make their financial commitment *to God through the Church during all the worship services.* Because pledging is a covenant between every person and God, pledging will be done in church. Pledge cards will be available and time will be provided, following the sermon, to sign the cards. Our pledges will then be collected and offered to God at the Altar as part of our spiritual covenant for 1975. Those who do not pledge in church will be called on by a steward on that afternoon. Hopefully, by that evening, the program will be 95 percent complete.

5. One week later, on the following Sunday, November 5, the pledge totals will be turned over to the Finance Committee so they can prepare our budget for 1975.

6. Tentative budget proposals will be presented for the discussion of the whole parish at the coffee hours on November 12 and 19. Then, a clear budget proposal will be made in total at the Epiphany Dinner in January, for final action by the whole parish.

Exhibit 2   Second example of first mailing

                              To be used in Week One

(Church letterhead)

October 25, 1974

THIS IS A SPECIAL COMMUNICATION
ABOUT A VERY SPECIAL MATTER

It isn't often that communications from your Church come in envelopes marked IMPORTANT MAIL. This one does because we wanted it set apart from everything else. It is IMPORTANT MAIL in the best sense of that term.

IT HAS TO DO WITH OUR FALL
STEWARDSHIP PROGRAM.

Your Church invites and needs you to participate in the life of your Church, especially . . .

ON THREE SUNDAYS:

NOVEMBER 4   NOVEMBER 11   NOVEMBER 18

On these three Sundays, the whole Church will be praying for our EVERY MEMBER CANVASS for 1975.

It is said that "more things are wrought by prayer than this world knows of." We believe that, and we deeply want you to join us in praying for this important thrust in our parish life.

On these same three Sundays, the rector will also be

preaching three sermons around a stewardship theme. The sermon titles will be:

NOVEMBER 4	"And Why *Should* I Give?"
NOVEMBER 11	"What in the World Are We Doing Here?"
NOVEMBER 18	"On Knowing Where to Draw the Line"

During these same three weeks—in the Epistle—written material will be sent to you on the subject of stewardship, to describe both a philosophy of Christian stewardship and the mechanics of our program. A statement of this philosophy is included in this envelope.

On Sunday, November 18, you and your family, together with all Saint Stephenites, will be invited to make your financial commitment to God through the Church during all of our worship services. Because pledging is a covenant between each person and God, pledging will be done, as we did last year, as a part of our worship. Pledge cards will be available and time will be provided following the sermon to sign the cards. Our pledges will then be collected and offered to God at the altar as part of our spiritual covenant for 1975. Those who prefer not to pledge in church will be called on by a steward on that afternoon. Hopefully, by that evening, the program will be 95 percent complete.

Incidentally, prior to this Sunday, November 4, you will be contacted (along with every other parish family) by the steward who has your card. He or she will describe our program plans for this fall and especially invite you to attend church on these three consecutive Sundays: November 4, 11, and 18. He or she will also invite your prayers for and comments about Saint Stephen's Church. Every family will have an opportunity to talk with one of these seventy parish leaders as the program begins.

So, why is this IMPORTANT MAIL?
Because it invites you . . .
   to join us in worship . . .
     to pray for our Every Member Canvass . . .
      to participate in a vital program in your Church.
Thank you for reading this right to the end!
Be with us because you can make a difference!

                In Christ,

                _____

                Rector

                _____

                Senior Warden

                _____

                Canvass Chairperson

The steward who will be calling you is your fellow church member.

                _____

Exhibit 3

STEWARDSHIP—THE QUESTION IS "WHY?"

In an old-time evangelical church, the preacher was warming up to his sermon topic on stewardship, and he said, "The Church has got to get up and run!" And the people shouted, "Amen." The preacher went on, "And the Church has got to rise up and fly!" And the people shouted, "Praise the Lord." The preacher continued, "If the Church is going to run and fly, it's got to have money." And the congregation groaned, "Let's walk!"

In the Church, while more and more Christians are becoming more and more committed givers in our time, the subject nonetheless tends to raise the hair on the back of our necks, and we say, "Ooh, that again!"

Part of the reason for this response at stewardship time may well be that we ask ourselves the wrong questions. We ask, "How much should I give?" A more primary question, and a better one, might be, "Why should I give anything at all in support of the Church? Such a question deserves a good answer.

For Christians, there is a way of answering that is basically and fundamentally a religious act.

And our way of answering is to say that we need to give because we have been given to. Stop and consider all that you have, all that you have been given as a gift. Take a minute and make a list. It might include the following things:

1. Life and health, given as a pure act of God.

2. A good earth in which to live out our life, put here for us as an act of God.

3. Raw materials in the earth to use and develop and create from, to make life good and better-than-good for ourselves and others.

4. A brain to think with, a body to work with, a talent to develop into something useful and beautiful, and a wide variety of opportunities in which to use the things we have been given.

5. And most important of all, we have been given Jesus Christ, a Savior who is able to rejoice with us when we use these gifts well, and to forgive us when we use these gifts poorly.

Now, to be sure, people vary tremendously in what each will make out of these gifts, and our success in using what we have been given is, in large measure, determined by the effort and work we are willing to expend. And, praise God, some have done very well. But the gifts we have in the beginning remain gifts, something we have for which we are fundamentally not responsible. God is the giver. We are the users of God's gifts.

So why should any one of us ever give anything to God? We *need* to give, out of thanksgiving for all these things that we have been given to use. We don't need to give so much out of what we "own," as we need to share, in thanksgiving, out of what we have given.

We believe that this is the basic difference between raising money for the Church, an admirable goal, and practicing stewardship with God, a basically religious goal. Our very deep hope at Saint Stephen's this fall is that we can become sharers more than givers, stewards with God more than money raisers with the Church.

Exhibit 4   Second example of
                           statement of stewardship theology

                              To be used in Week Two

                              *(This piece is designed as a
                         four-page folder and includes the material
                            on pages 79 to 83 as a single piece.)*

Folder—Page 1

THE STORY OF A MAN . . .

AND HIS LIFE . . .

AND A DREAM . . .

Folder—Page 2

George and Mary Churchmember were fine people,
the kind anyone would want for friends. They were
members of Saint Stephen's Church.

It happened that one night, after a dinner party, full of
good food, and fellowship, George and Mary retired for
a good night's rest. But George began to dream.

The Church was beginning its Every Member Canvass
program and a steward from the Church was standing

with George in his living room. Strangely, the face of his caller was familiar, but above his head was the faintest hint of a halo and behind his back, like two humps, was the faintest outline of two wings.

Now George had always signed a pledge card, depending on what he could afford to give. And when the Church was in need, he sometimes added a little, because he thought the Church was a good thing.

But in his dream, much to his own amazement, George began to argue with his caller. And it was violent.

"Now you tell me," he said, "why should I give anything at all to the Church?"

The violence of the question made George roll over on his bed.

"You give because you have been given to," was the almost kindly reply.

"But what have I been given?" George responded angrily. "What I have, I have earned by darn hard work."

And then it happened, as it sometimes does in dreams, that right where his fireplace should have been, there appeared a huge sheet of white paper. And, as if by some unspoken command, a hand began to write. The first words were:

THINK AND CONSIDER

George was so fascinated watching the hand that he did not reply, and the hand moved again. It wrote:

A LIFE TO LIVE

HEALTH TO LIVE BY

THE EARTH TO LIVE IN

"Well," George said, "that's true; those are gifts, but I didn't mean those things."

And again the hand wrote:

THEN THINK AND CONSIDER

And the hand went on:

THE RAW MATERIALS TO CREATE WITH

A BRAIN TO THINK WITH

A BODY TO WORK WITH

"Well, all right, those too, are gifts, but I didn't mean . . ." His words were stopped in mid-air as the hand went on:

WAIT

Then:

PERSONAL TALENTS TO USE

THE OPPORTUNITIES TO USE THEM

That was the time (as George remembered his dream) that he sat down. And, as he was sitting, the hand had written:

ALL GIFTS, GEORGE, ALL GIFTS

Folder—Page 4

Then everything disappeared from the sheet but one word:

WHERE?

"Do you mean where do all these things come from?" Now, George was a good man. And he knew where. So he rose and went to the paper and he wrote one word:

GOD

And then, the hand wrote again:

AND WHAT ELSE, GEORGE?

Now, besides being a good man, George was also a smart man. So he began to think, and then, almost hesitantly, he wrote:

PRAYER IN NEED

FORGIVENESS IN ERROR

STRENGTH IN WEAKNESS

Now George really believed these things, had experienced these things, although he was not too comfortable talking about them. But even as these thoughts passed through his mind, he was writing:

JESUS CHRIST, A GIFT OF GOD

And that's when George woke up.

That week, nothing much happened to George, until one day he received a letter from the Church. It was about the Every Member Canvass.

He didn't read it very carefully, but one paragraph caught his attention:

So, why should anyone of us give anything to God? We give because we have already been given to. We give because we need to give out of thanksgiving for all the things we have been given to use. We believe *that* attitude is the difference between raising money for the Church and practicing Christian stewardship with God.

And, out loud, George said, "Yes."
"What did you say?" Mary asked him.
"Oh," George replied, "I was just remembering a dream I had last week."

Exhibit 5

STEWARDSHIP—THE QUESTION IS "HOW?"

For the past two weeks, we have tried, in this Epistle, to say something about a philosophy of stewardship. The first week we spoke about WHY a Christian gives. We give because we have been given to.

Then we said that the effect of our giving or sharing is as strong on the giver as it is on the receiver. Satisfaction and a sense of well-being seem to come to those who share openly, in a way that those who do not share don't seem to experience.

But those things don't answer the pragmatic questions. Most of us are givers or are honestly convinced that we should be. The question is how to know what to give.

There is one way to consider your giving that we seriously commend to your thought. It's called PROPORTIONATE GIVING. If we give because we have been given to, then we will want to give from what we have; that is, in relation to our income.

Christian sharing is to share a worthy proportion of our income with God through the Church. If we are conscientious stewards, then we don't want to play games with God. Proportionate giving helps us to know clearly what we are giving in relation to what we have.

For example:

If your family income is $30,000 annually and you pledge $17 a week to God through the Church, then it is helpful to know that that represents about 3 percent of your income.

If your family income is $15,000 annually and you pledge $8.50 a week to God through the Church, that also represents 3 percent of your income.

If your family income is $20,000 annually and you give $5 a week to God through the Church, that represents just over 1 percent of your income.

Proportionate giving allows you to keep your pledge between yourself and God. It puts the spotlight on the giver and his relationship with God.

Many Christians begin their giving with a modern tithe; that is, 5 percent of their income to God, through the Church, and 5 percent to other charities of their own choice.

Many give more than that. Others, while they are not able to make a 5 percent tithe all at once, are beginning at 3 percent and increasing the percentage of their gift each year.

Whatever percentage you may be able to consider, proportionate giving is one way for every parish family to:
- Give honestly and conscientiously of what we have
- Be honest with God
- Be honest with ourselves

As you consider your pledge, we commend it to your serious Christian consideration.

Exhibit 6   Example of fourth mailing

To be used in Week Four

STEWARDSHIP—THE QUESTION IS "HOW MUCH?"

How long has it been since you measured your giving? Have you done so recently?

When did you last figure just *what* your giving really amounts to?

What percentage of your income for 1974 are we really sharing with God, through the work of Saint Stephen's Church?

You can figure it out very easily. For example:

If your income for 1974 is $25,000 and your pledge to God through Saint Stephen's is $5 a week, then that gift represents about 1 percent of your income.

You see, when you measure your gift in that way, you don't fool yourself about your sharing. You don't measure yourself against what others who may have less to give from are giving . . . nor do you measure yourself against others who seem to have so much more to give from.

Proportionate giving provides you with a way to measure yourself against yourself . . . what you give against what you have. This year, we are inviting every family at Saint Stephen's to consider giving in this manner; giving from income, sharing from what we have with God through Saint Stephen's parish. This is called proportionate giving.

Some illustrations might help. For example:

a. If, in 1974, you gave $10 a week and want to become a proportionate giver, then simply divide your gift ($520 annually) by your income and see what percentage of your income your gift represents; then determine what you would like to share and adjust your weekly pledge to meet that percentage.

b. If, in 1974, you gave $300 and now you want to become a proportionate giver, then simply divide your gift ($300) by your income and see what percentage of your income your gift represents; then determine what percentage you would like to give and adjust your gift to meet that percentage.

"Chance giving," that is, giving what we can without much commitment or effort required, is about 1 percent of income.

With an awareness of Christian stewardship, giving will move up to 3 percent.

Committed giving begins at about $1 a week for each $1,000 of annual income ($50 annually for each $1,000 of annual income) or roughly 5 percent of income. This is called the modern tithe.

The biblical guideline, which would include all our giving in and out of the Church, remains at 10 percent. Sacrificial giving begins here and goes out.

The percentage you use is less important than the fact that you conscientiously make a measure. You can't fool God. So why try to fool yourself?

The chart below suggests the simple results of the formula above. It might be helpful as you consider your pledge. It is here for your information only.

A Guide to Proportionate Giving

IF YOUR ANNUAL GROSS INCOME IS:	YOUR PROPORTIONATE WEEKLY GIFT WOULD BE:				
	3%	4%	5%	10%	12%
$ 8,000	$ 4.62	$ 6.15	$ 7.70	$15.40	$ 18.46
9,000					
10,000					
12,000					
15,000					
17,500					
20,000					
50,000	26.92	38.46	48.00	96.00	115.38

SECTION TWO

Examples of sermons that could be used according to the schedule suggested in Chapter 4. The concepts illustrated in sermons may be used as suggested or combined and adapted to a shorter or longer campaign. All the sermons have been preached by this writer in his own parish.

Exhibit 7

A SERMON ON STEWARDSHIP THEOLOGY

This morning we are beginning something which might be termed the most important spiritual adventure we have undertaken for some time. Beginning today, and continuing for the next three weeks, we are going to be engaged in our annual stewardship program. And, to help us all consider our stewardship in a spiritual framework, where we believe it belongs, we are going to try to do several things in these next three weeks. Each week specific information on our program will be printed in our Epistle along with some comments about a uniquely Christian philosophy of sharing or giving. The last two Epistles have carried this information on a separate insert sheet, and the next two, we hope, will amplify these things more fully. In addition, personal telephone contacts are being made with every family in our parish by appointed stewards, fellow members of our parish. And we hope that at the coffee hour following this service, you and your steward will get together and meet each other face to face. And all this will come to a climax on Sunday, October 29th, when every family in this parish will be invited to make a financial commitment to God through this Church. On that day, immediately following the sermon, while we are right here in our pews, an opportunity will be given to make your commitment to God on a pledge card.

These cards will then be gathered and joyfully offered to God on the altar. For those who do not pledge during our worship, on that afternoon, October 29th, these seventy stewards will go out into all homes to talk about sharing and to receive your pledges for 1975. Hopefully, by the evening of October 29th, we will be substantially finished, so we can then turn, and joyfully so, to translating these financial commitments we have made into a budget for our parish for the coming year.

And, also, in these three weeks, our sermons will be given to a consideration of stewardship . . . what it means to be a Christian steward . . . where the Church ought to be and *could* be . . . and how we all can be a part of that. This morning, we want to think (I hope, somewhat directly) about ourselves as stewards; next week we will try to speak about the Church and maybe even dream a little about the potential and possibilities that are here; and on October 29th, we will want to think about Christian giving under the title, "The Subject Jesus Talked about Most."

So . . . this process begins this morning. We begin by thinking some about ourselves. And the text, if indeed we need a text, comes from the twenty-fifth chapter of the Gospel of Saint Matthew. You remember the story, as we read it for our Second Lesson this morning.

A man was about to travel into a far country, and so he called his servants together to put them in charge of his property. To one he gave five talents; to another, two talents; and to a third, one talent. And you remember, too, that each of these did well with their holding—each one doubling what he had been given, except the last. The one-talent man, fearful that he might lose what he was given, buried his talent in the ground, doing nothing with it. And, as the parable ends, the owner returns to reward the faithful servants. The unfaithful servant was severely judged, and the one talent he had been given was taken away. That's the story in the twenty-fifth chapter of Saint Matthew.

Now, I've read that story many times, as you have, and I've often felt badly about the poor one-talent man. He *really* took his lumps. He didn't seem to have as much to work with as the others, and I guess I have tried to excuse him on that account. But the point of the parable is not how many talents each man was given. There is one much more significant point that seems germane, both to the parable and to our subject this morning. The point I would like to ask you to consider is this: The parable suggests that what we have, we have because it has been given to us by God.

"A man, going on a journey, called his servants and entrusted to them his property."

Of course, the man is God and we are the servants to whom a great many things have been given. Life and breath, a good earth in which to live, and a considerable space of time in which to *do* something with what we have been given. Over and over again, in both the Old and the New Testaments, is this theme of God's ownership of all things and our partnership in all things emphasized. "The earth is the Lord's and fullness thereof." That's from the first book of the Chronicles.

And, in a more familiar verse, "All things come of thee, O Lord, and of thine own have we given thee."

Or again, "Thine, O Lord, is the greatness, and the power, and the glory, and the victory, and the majesty; for all that is in the heavens and in the earth is thine."

It's a basic tenet of the Hebrew-Christian faith. What we have, we have because it has been *given* to us.

Now, we can refine that in a hundred ways.

Not too many years ago, the Associated Press released a study done by an agricultural school in Iowa. It reported that production of 100 bushels of corn from one acre of land, in addition to the many hours of the farmer's labor, required 4,000,000 pounds of water, 6,800 pounds of oxygen, 5,200 pounds of carbon, 160 pounds of nitrogen, 125 pounds of potassium, 75 pounds of yellow sulfur, and other elements too numerous to list. And, in addition to these things, which no man can produce by himself, the right amount of rain and heat is crucial, and man also has no control over these things. It was estimated, the report said, that only 5 percent of the produce of a farm can be attributed to man's efforts. Of course, neither the Associated Press nor any state college could overtly identify the source of the other 95 percent. But someone else once wrote about the same idea and, in a little verse, identified the source:

> Back of the loaf is the snowy flour,
> And back of the flour, the mill.
> And back of the mill are the wheat and showers
> And the sun and the Father's will."
> "All things come of thee, O Lord . . ."

Many years ago, a Louisiana law firm was asked to undertake a title search for some property in New Orleans. They successfully traced the title back to the Louisiana Purchase in 1803. But their clients were not satisfied with that. And so the search went on, and finally the law firm wrote the following letter to their client:

Gentlemen:

Please be advised that in the year 1803, the United States of America acquired the territory of Louisiana from the Republic of France, by purchase. The Republic of France, in turn, acquired title from the Spanish Crown by conquest; the Spanish Crown having obtained it by virtue of the discoveries of one Christopher Columbus, who had been authorized to undertake his journey by Isabella, Queen of Spain, who obtained sanction for the voyage from the Pope, the Vicar of Christ, who is the son and heir of Almighty God, who made Louisiana.

And without our going back that far, we already know that what we are accustomed to call our own is not really ours. It is God's. And what we do is just hold it for awhile, use it, maybe add to it, and then pass it on. God is the owner. We are the partners. "A man going on a journey called his servants and entrusted to them his property."

But, again, it's not quite as simple as that. There is a story that adds another dimension to what we are trying to say this morning.

A minister once went out to visit one of his members. He lived in a run-down house with a front yard that was a real tangle of weeds and brush and tall grass. But over a few months, the man had literally transformed that front yard into a beautiful lawn and garden. When the minister called, he saw the wondrous improvement, and he said to the man, "My, isn't it wonderful what you and God have done to this yard?" And the man replied, "Yes, it is. But you should have seen it when God had it alone."

This story points up the obvious fact that much of what we have, we have because we have worked for it, because we have invested our time and effort and enthusiasm and money to be where we are right now. And it's out of this very sharp awareness of our sweat and toil that many people claim a pride of ownership, a pride of accomplishment, and so easily say, "Look at what I've done!" And there is no question about it . . . for many hard-working people, that's the simple truth as far as it goes. We have what we have because we have worked very hard for it. But for a Christian, pride of accomplishment just isn't that superficial.

A Christian is able to go beneath that. What we are, what we have been able to do, we have done because we have been the recipients of boundless gifts. A life to live; we didn't earn that. A brain to think with, a talent to use; these things we have not earned. Indeed, isn't that something of what life is all about—to take what we have been given, to use it, to develop it, and from it to produce something of value, something of beauty in this world.

And it goes deeper than just that, too. Not life and breath and talent alone, but God has given us so much more. A way to find direction and strength, a way we call prayer. A way to grow in love and forgiveness and power to live, a way we call Sacraments. A way to see life in this world and the next, and not as a stranger but as a Son of the Most High God—a way provided through Jesus Christ. And whether we fully use or even fully recognize these gifts, they are ours, that our life may be potentially rich and full and beautiful. Jesus used the word *abundant.* And we haven't earned a single one of these gifts. No one who thinks deeply at all can stop when he says, "Look at what I've done." He goes on to say, "Look at what I've done with what God has given me."

And what has all that to do with our stewardship? Simply this: When we, in our turn, consider our own giving, we consider it best when we see it as a response to the Giver, and, as an act of Thankgiving, return to Him out of what we have earned. There is a fundamental difference between giving out of what we own to help some worthy cause, and sharing out of what we have been given out of our Thanksgiving. The first is called philanthropy. The second is called Christian stewardship.

And maybe another difference between the two is that, in the first, we tend to give only our money. In the second we are more likely to be able to give ourselves. And maybe that's really what the parable of the talents is all about. Having been given gifts, two men used them so as to be able to have something extra, something of themselves, to return to the Giver. The third man withheld himself and returned only what he had been given, unused and undeveloped.

And it was only to the first two that the Giver was able to say, "Well done, thou good and faithful servant."

Let us pray:

Almighty God, whose loving hand has given us all that we possess: grant us grace that we may honor you with our substance. Help us to see that we are unworthy of your blessings, unless we share them with others. Bless our effort in this Every Member Canvass, and remembering the account we must one day give, help us as people and parish to be faithful stewards of your bounty, through Jesus Christ our Lord. Amen.

Exhibit 8

This morning we enter the second week of our three-week stewardship program here at our parish. Next Sunday, in our third week, every family in the parish will be invited to make their financial commitment to God through this church for 1975. Pledging will be done right here, in the church, immediately following the sermon. And then, on that afternoon (next Sunday), seventy stewards will go out to call on those who have not yet pledged. By the following Sunday we hope to have the entire program complete and to be able to go to work on whatever budget our financial commitments allow us to create.

Last Sunday we tried to emphasize the fact that what we are accustomed to call our own is not really ours, but God's. To be sure, what we have, we have in part because we have earned it. But we have not said enough when we say, "Look at what I have done." It's only enough when we are able to say, "Look at what I have done with what God has given me."

This week we want to come a little closer to home and think some about the Church and especially about our parish church. And, while we do have some very real needs (needs to pay people; needs to provide adequate equipment and to support programs, inside and outside our parish; needs to maintain these lovely buildings; needs which we depend wholly and totally on your sharing in order to meet), these are not the things we want directly to think about this morning. This morning I'd like to dream a little about the parish and about some things that, hopefully, might widen our vision about what there is to do, what we could do, as a Christian congregation.

To do that, I'd like to tell you two stories. Both of them are true. Both of them are incidents that I know, from first hand, having been directly involved in them.

The first took place in Africa in a small, unknown country called Ovamboland. The young man's name is not important. Because it was almost unpronounceable by the American tongue, we called him "Chester." We learned about Chester through a missionary. He was a bushman, one of those wild-looking hairy people sometimes pictured on the cover of National Geographic. But Chester was not a picture. Chester was a man—a man with real feelings, with real dreams of his own—a man who loved his wife and worried about his children. And Chester was sick, very sick. But Chester didn't know what was wrong. All he knew was that he no longer felt as strong as he did before, and that pain was increasingly becoming a regular part of every day. The witch doctors in the bush did what they could, which was nothing. His wife did what she could, which was nothing. And Chester did what he could, which was nothing. And the disease became progressively worse—until one day, Chester remembered the missionary. A little bush station had been built by a team of three Episcopalians: a priest, a doctor, and a nurse. And from that lean-to made of sticks, stories of great miracles of healing were coming back. And one day Chester walked thirty-seven miles from his village to that lean-to, looking for a miracle to relieve his pain. His disease was diagnosed as tuberculosis, and Chester was taken to the main mission station for surgery and treatment. Oh yes, Chester was made whole again, completely cured by surgery. But that's not the point of the story. You see, Chester was also a very intelligent man, very bright. And while he recuperated, Chester also went to school for the first time in his life. A mud brick school had been built with money given by a Christian congregation in Minnesota. And the same congregation had provided money to pay a native teacher. It took Chester nine months to go through the first six grades, at least by Ovambo standards. And, vastly more important, the teacher was also a Christian. And Chester, also for the first time in his life, learned about a God who loved him and about Jesus Christ who died for him. Well, Chester went home healed of his disease, and a baptized Christian. And we would not know much about Chester except that, within the next year, he was back—and back with his entire family—to live. You see, Chester wanted to be a priest. Chester wanted to be trained to learn everything that he could so he could take this God back to his own village and teach them. The last I knew of him, Chester was in high school and enrolled for the next class in the small, shabby, pitifully inadequate, but magnificent, seminary in backward Ovamboland. And how do I know all these things? Because I was in the parish that built that school. And Chester wrote us a letter to thank us for his education, a letter in which he also expressed his faith in God—a faith, the warmth of which, even on paper, put my own faith to shame. That was ten years ago. And sometimes, when I dream about what the Church could do, I think of Chester and thousands of others like him. And I dream that maybe, again, there will be a parish that has a vision wide enough to do something like that again, to bring God to someone else, like him, somewhere else in the world.

You know, Jesus told a parable about people like Chester. In the thirteenth chapter of Saint Matthew's Gospel, Jesus tells a series of parables about the spread of the Kingdom of God. And he talks about the different kinds of responses men will make to the proclamation of God's word. "Some seed will fall on the path and never take root," he says. "Other seeds will fall on rocky ground and will grow, but without deep enough roots to sustain life. Still others will take root, but will be choked by so many other things that they will never bear fruit. But some will produce grain a hundredfold." Surely, Chester has produced grain a hundredfold.

But the significant thing in what Jesus says, in our context this morning, comes later in the chapter. His disciples came to him and asked him to explain the parable of the soils. And Jesus begins the explanation by saying, "The field is the world." And, indeed, it is. For any parish church, "the field is the world." And when I dream, I do dream that maybe there will, again, be a parish that has a vision wide enough, a concern strong enough, the resources big enough, to bring a God like that to others like Chester, somewhere else in the world.

But that's not the only thing I dream about. Let me tell you another story. It's about a girl. We'll call her Cynthia. And her story is not like Chester's at all. Cynthia lived in a suburban village and attended high school there. She was not a good student, and that was a source of constant irritation to her parents. But she got by because she was moderately pretty and a very fast talker. And, as she grew, that was not all that was fast about her. She and her family were members of our parish. I didn't know any of them very well, until one day I met her. She had been picked up by the police with a sizable load of clothing she and her friends had tried to steal from a large suburban department store. She was a thief, but she was not a thief. She was mostly a lonely, scared child in trouble, way over her head. Well, I did what

I could. There were hours of counseling with her, and with her parents, and with her and her parents, together. And when that made no progress, there were psychologists who worked with her. And when that didn't seem to work, there was group counseling in a "far out" kind of youth center. And when that didn't work, she was sent away from home to try to break her out of the environment of friends and neighborhood and family that seemed to chain her up so deeply. At this moment, as I tell you this, I don't know if that's going to work. But I do know that, somehow, all of this was necessary.

While many people were desperately concerned about her, our concern came very much too late. And I have often wondered what might have been if all of us had been this concerned about her some years before when she was still what we could call "a good girl." What if the Church had been able to provide the resources and the people and a strong enough youth program to reach out to her, to reinforce her, when reinforcing her goodness might have made a difference. Maybe it would not have mattered. But we'll never know because we were *not* able to do that. Now, I don't fault the Church for that failure, nor do I assume that our inability was the only factor in what happened to her. But when I dream about the Church, I dream of a parish that *is* able and willing to provide these things. A strong youth ministry can do much to help the kids in trouble. It can do infinitely more to support and work with kids *before* they get in trouble, so that maybe that kind of trouble doesn't even become a possibility.

Well, I dream other dreams, too, about our Church. To the west of us there are two areas growing rapidly with bright population futures: Eden Prairie and Jonathan. There are no Episcopal churches in either place. I dream that Saint Stephen's, along with the diocese of Minnesota and other parishes in our region, might provide the resources to start a ministry in one or both of these places.

But all my dreams are not as specific as that. Sometimes I dream about our vestry, that these dedicated men and women should not have to spend all their time and energy robbing Peter to pay Paul, in our parish budget, but can spend time dreaming, too, about things we *could* and *should* do, because we *do* have the resources to do them.

Recently, I received a mimeographed sheet from a medical group. It described a series of programs this group was sponsoring all over the world. A nurse was being maintained in the Dominican Republic; a general practitioner was supported in Afghanistan; a medical-dental team had been established in Tunisia; a surgeon was maintained in Viet Nam; and, in addition to these things, there was a strong plea for a G.P. or pediatrician to work in public health in Nicaragua. Attached to this report, sent by a doctor friend of mine, was a note on a prescription pad. It read, "John, what would happen to the Church if it took its sense of mission with this degree of serious commitment and enthusiasm? Something to think about!"

And mostly, I guess, I *do* dream about this parish, hoping that we all will have the vision to look beyond the simple maintenance of what we are, into the creation of what we might be and could be, as a Church.

And maybe all this could be summed up in this way:

Not so many years ago, there was a program on television called "The Millionaire." Maybe some of you remember it. Each week, in the program, someone was given a gift of a million dollars. And the program was centered on what each individual did with it and what happened to the people who suddenly had all that money.

Well, I don't expect that anyone is going to give us a million dollars, but what would we do if we *did* have more than we needed simply to maintain what we are now trying to do? Now, there is something we could all dream about. And maybe that's not all that big a dream.

Let us pray:

Almighty God, whose loving hand has given us all that we possess: grant us grace that we may honor you with our substance. Help us to see that we are unworthy of your blessings, unless we share them with others. Bless our effort in this Every Member Canvass, and remembering the account we must one day give, help us as people and parish to be faithful stewards of your bounty, through Jesus Christ our Lord. Amen.

Exhibit 9

SERMON FOR PLEDGE SUNDAY

This morning we have finally come to the day toward which we have been building for some time. Today is Pledge Day here at our parish. This is the day on which all of us are invited to make our financial commitment to God through this Church.

Pledging will be done in just a few minutes while we remain right here in our pews. Then our gifts will be taken up to the Altar and offered directly to God in a special offertory. And then, this afternoon, following our services, stewards will go out to call on every family in this parish who has not yet pledged. By 6:00 P.M. tonight we hope to have our stewardship program 90 percent complete, and by next Sunday, we hope to be able to turn our final pledge totals over to our finance committee to begin preparing a budget for 1975.

So this, then, is Pledge Day and this is called the "Money Sermon."

Now, I suppose, if I were to be as realistic as possible about this, the best place to begin such a sermon would be to recognize that, for some people, including many preachers, the money sermon is a little bit distasteful—a little crass—necessary, but not really very nice. It's a little like the evangelical preacher who was warming up to his subject one morning, bringing his congregation along with him. "Brethren," he said, "the Church is going to rise up and run." And the congregation chorused, "Amen." "Brethren, the Church is going to rise up and fly." And the congregation shouted, "Hallelujah." "Brethren, for the Church to run and to fly, it's going to take money!" And the old deacon in the front row slumped down and mumbled, "Amen, brother, let's walk."

With a money sermon, there does seem to come to some people a kind of a reluctance to hear and to seriously consider our giving as a spiritual concern. To be honest with you, there was a time when I shared that reluctance. I mean, to preach on love and prayer and being kind was one thing, but *money* in the *pulpit?* Then one day someone suggested something to me that I have since checked out and found, to my very great surprise, to be true. While I was hesitant to talk about money in the church, Jesus showed no such hesitation. While congregations sometimes consider the subject of money a "touchy" one, Jesus never hesitated to speak of it. In fact, with a little research, I discovered that well over one-third of all the parables in the New Testament are directly concerned with our possessions. And in the four Gospels, that record of the words of Jesus, over one-sixth of all the verses in those Gospels talk about our possessions and how they should be used. The fact is that, of all the things Jesus talked about, the subject he talked about most was the relationship of a man and his money.

And of all of the things Jesus said, there are two themes that appear over and over again.

For the past two Sundays we have tried to speak to one of them. We have tried to say that what we have, we have because it has been given to us. Life, breath, a talent, a skill to use, a good earth in which to use what we have—these have all been given to us. And not these alone, but there are other things—less tangible things—that we have been given. Things like prayer, and sacraments, as ways of reaching out to God who is also reaching out to us. These, too, we haven't earned, but they have been given. And all this we tried to tie up by suggesting that we are like the servants in the parable of the talents. "A man, going on a journey, called his servants and entrusted to them his property." And that theme is followed by a second theme of Jesus, one on which I would like to spend a few minutes this morning.

And, simply stated, it is this: the primary values of your life—the things you really cherish and value the most, indeed, the kind of people you are—will be reflected in the way you *use* your possessions.

I think that is one of the most important reasons Jesus spent so much time talking about a man and his money. Jesus knew that the real key to a man's character—the key to what a person really is like—is in how he uses his possessions. Someone once said, "The way to judge a man's religion is not in questioning what he thinks about Jesus Christ, but in questioning what he thinks about his property." And a writer of historical biography one time said the same thing when he said, "Show me where a man spends his money, and I will show you the real man." And Jesus himself, put it best when, according to the sixth chapter of Saint Matthew's Gospel, he said, "for where your *treasure* is, *there* shall your heart be also."

And Jesus illustrated this in many ways. In the twelfth chapter of Saint Mark's Gospel, Jesus was standing at the door of the temple and saw how many came and gave their offerings. And some gave substantial amounts because they *had* much, but a widow came and gave two mites—a very small offering—but it was *all* that she had. And Jesus called his disciples to him and commended the widow for her gift. And not because it was going to do much for the temple, or because it was so big, but because, in relation to what she had, it suggested so much of what her values were—what kind of a person she really was.

And, by contrast, the thing that roused Jesus to come to his hottest peak of exasperation was when people—honest, upright, respectable people—refused to look beyond the borders of their own comfortable existence and did not share, thankfully, out of what they had: Dives—the rich man who day after day walked past Lazarus, who was begging at his gate; the rich farmer, who, with a bumper crop, could think of nothing to do with it but to build bigger barns to store it. And it wasn't their failure to help someone that primarily bothered Jesus; it was that their actions revealed so much about what they *really* valued—about what kind of people they really were.

Bruce Barton, who wrote the book *The Man Nobody Knows*, tells about the two seas in Palestine. One is fresh and clear and it's filled with fish. Splashes of green adorn its banks. Trees abound and children play on sandy beaches, beside the blue and clean waters. This is the Sea of Galilee. To the north, the Jordan River flows into it, and to the south, the Jordan River flows out of it.

Farther south, there is another sea. The Jordan flows into it also. But here there is no splash of fish, no green abounding, no trees, and no children playing on its banks. The air hangs heavy over the sea and no one drinks of its acid-like water.

And what is the difference between the two seas? This is the difference: The Sea of Galilee receives, but does not keep, the Jordan River; for every drop that flows in, another is given out. But the other sea is smarter than that. The Jordan flows in, but it does *not* flow out, there are no springs flowing out. Every drop it gets, it keeps. The Sea of Galilee gives and lives. The other sea gives nothing. It is named the Dead Sea.

And maybe the same point is made by these words: "You make a *living* by what you earn; you make a *life* by what you give."

Jesus was right. The primary values of our life—the things we *really* think are important, the kind of people we really are—will be reflected by the way in which we use our possessions.

And I guess that leads us right to the heart of the issue. If what we are saying is true, then how do we translate that into our giving? Well, the Christian translation can be stated very briefly. It is called proportionate giving. And, very simply, it goes like this:

If, indeed, what we have, we have because it has been given—and if, indeed, the things we really value are revealed by how we use what we've been given—then what do those things suggest about our own giving to God through the Church? The question is never "What does the Church need?" but rather "How much do I have, from which I can share?" Giving becomes a responsibly figured percentage of your income—not a percent of the Church's budget, but a percentage of our income, honestly computed. The Christian standard of giving begins at 5 percent of income. Many should give more than that, and indeed there are those in this parish who do give more than that. And if there are those who can't consider 5 percent, then 4 percent or 3 percent. But whatever it is, proportionate giving asks you to stop and think about it this way: A gift to God is a gift in thanksgiving, carefully thought out and honestly figured, from our income.

I saw something the other day in connection with proportionate giving that really amazed me. Someone figured out that if every Episcopal family in the country were suddenly made destitute and all of us went on Social Security at the lowest family level, and then if all of us, at that income level, gave 5 percent to the Church, the income of the Church for God's work, would increase seven times over what it is. That's the power of proportionate giving. And it makes me wonder what might be possible in this parish if every family—every individual with income—would sign a pledge card today for 5 percent or 4 percent or even 3 percent. Maybe some of the dreams we dream would then come true.

And maybe all this can be summed up in a little story.

One rainy afternoon, two children were trying to entertain themselves inside when one hit on the idea of acting out their Sunday School lesson of the morning. It was the story of Noah and the flood. And so, they found a cardboard box to be the ark and up to the bathroom they ran. The shower became the rains, and soon the flood covered the bottom of the tub and the ark began to float. It was a great flood. And after some time, they turned off the shower and the rains ceased and the ark floated on the water. They pushed the wall switch and the sun reappeared. They pulled the plug in the bathtub, and the floods descended until the ark once more rested on dry ground. There was another part of the story, however. Noah and his wife had offered a sacrifice to God. And so the children decided the kitchen stove would be the place for them to burn their sacrifice. And reaching into the ark, the little boy found one of his sister's animals and said, "Let's burn this—it would make a good gift for God." "Oh, no," said his sister in pain. "I couldn't possibly part with that." And then, reaching into the ark, she found one of her brother's animals and said, "Here, let's give this to God instead." Her brother was unwilling to agree to that and they pondered for some time. And then the little girl had a happy thought. Scampering off to the attic, she returned in a few minutes with a little toy lamb. It had only three legs, its head was smashed, it had no tail, and it was so dirty no one could have guessed its original color. "Here," she cried, "let's give this to God." And the discarded, broken lamb that no one wanted was given as their sacrifice to God.

Now, these are children and this is a story. And of course we are not like children.

Before you take your pledge card, may I ask you to join me in saying the stewardship prayer which is on the inside of your bulletin.

Let us pray:

Almighty God, whose loving hand has given us all that we possess: grant us grace that we may honor you with our substance. Help us to see that we are unworthy of your blessings, unless we share them with others. Bless our effort in this Every Member Canvass, and remembering the account we must one day give, help us as people and parish to be faithful stewards of your bounty, through Jesus Christ our Lord. Amen.

Exhibit 10

This morning I want to try to suggest two very simple ideas for your consideration.

As you are aware, I am sure, this is the first Sunday of our annual three week Stewardship program here at St. Stephen's. The details of the program are familiar to most of you by now. Beginning today and continuing for the next three weeks, in our Epistle, in our prayers here on Sunday and in our sermons, we are going to be talking about Christian giving. Two of the Epistle messages have already been sent, one in a special mailing labelled, "IMPORTANT MAIL."

There will be two more Epistles speaking to the whys and wherefores of the giving of a Christian person which I genuinely hope will capture your imaginations and thought.

And all this will be brought to a climax two weeks from today, when, as a part of all our worship services, an opportunity will be given for each family in our parish to make our financial commitments to God through this church. As we began to do last year, we will again be inviting your pledge immediately following the sermon on November 18th. On that day, your pledges and mine will be offered to God on the altar of this church.

This morning is also the first of three sermons that will attempt to deal with some aspects of Christian giving in the Church.

To begin all of that, I'd like to presume a little and tell you an experience I had several years ago that has profoundly affected my thinking about Stewardship and the implications of which I earnestly hope will become a part of your thinking as you consider your pledge in these next weeks.

It happened in another community about fifteen years ago. Along with a great many other people, I was invited to attend a dinner meeting. I went somewhat reluctantly and out of a sense of duty, because it was the bishop who had invited me. It was a meeting to launch a new national program to help major charities, churches, colleges and private schools get the kind of financial support they needed.

An eminent Protestant minister spoke, a very eloquent Jewish rabbi, and a distinguished Roman Catholic priest also spoke. And the presentation was capped by the national president of a private school association. They were all very well prepared. Charts were shown and statistics were liberally quoted, showing how massively little we give for religious, education and social-welfare institutions in comparison with what we spend on luxuries. The comparison was shocking.

It was all well done. The statistics were startling enough, the speeches inspirational enough. And yet, while I was there to learn to raise money in my church, I found myself not paying all that close attention to it.

In a groggy sort of way, I suppose my mind was trying to set up its defenses against all these massive statistics and their implied reflection on my generosity and that of my parish.

Then, the chairman of the whole program got up to summarize the evening.

Well, I couldn't have been more wrong. What he said

instead was like an electric shock to my sleepy system. And I remember his words almost exactly.

"It seems to me," he said, "that the important thing is not raising money, but getting people to give; not what the money does for the institution that gets it, but what it does for the people who give it. After all," he continued, "if it were just a matter of getting the money, the professional fund raisers have that down to a science. But what I hope is that in your fund raising efforts you can preserve for people the privilege of free-will giving." Well, there was more to it than that. But those are the words that stuck with me.

"The important thing is what giving does for the person who gives. What I hope is that you can preserve for people the privilege of free-will giving."

Well, I went home with that, and with a question I have been asking ever since. "What makes giving such a great privilege for me?" And the answers that have come to me are not mine, but the Bible's. And I'd like to suggest two of them briefly for your honest thought as we begin our Stewardship program here.

And the first is this.

Giving is a privilege for me because it is one way I can return to God out of all the things he has given me.

We say it so easily in the church. "All things come of thee, O Lord, and of thine own have we given thee." "Praise God from Whom all blessings flow." "The earth is the Lord's and the fullness thereof." And when we say these things, I'm sure we believe them. But I have the feeling that the words don't really get to us until we begin to break them down. What do we really have that we got from the Lord? Maybe your list would be something like mine.

The gift of life and breath. I am alive because God has given me life and continues to give me breath to sustain my life.

The good earth in which to live out my life, here before I came and here long after I am gone. This good earth is a gift to me as a place in which to live.

The raw materials of the earth to use, to develop, to create with, to make life good and better than good for myself and others.

And even inside of me, a brain to think with, a body to work with, a talent or two to develop into something useful.

All these gifts for which neither you nor I can claim responsibility.

And beyond these things, as we sit here in this church preparing for the Holy Communion, there are so many other things that come so easily to mind.

I find I come to the Holy Communion differently every time I come. Sometimes my need is for forgiveness and I find it at the altar. Sometimes my need is for simple strength to do what I have to do. And I find it in the sacrament. Sometimes I feel the need just to make some contact with God in a tangible way. And I can in the bread and wine that carries God's presence to me. And these things, too, are gifts, gifts of God given to me.

Now, to be sure, people will vary tremendously in what each of us will make out of these gifts. And our success, our growth in using what we have been given is in large measure determined by what each of us is willing to put into them, in terms of plain hard work and effort, or in terms of donations. And, praise God, some of us have done very well. But the gifts we have in the beginning remain gifts, things for which we are not fundamentally responsible. God is the giver. We are the users of God's gifts.

And what has all that to do with our giving? Maybe a homely little story will illustrate.

It seems there was a cow and pig who lived in the same

farmyard. They were good friends and one day the pig came to the cow with a problem.

"I don't know why the farmer treats you so well and me so badly," he said. "He has given you a name and feeds you every day with clean feed and he provides you with a clean dry stall to live in. But I don't have a name, and all I get to eat are the rotting scraps from his table and I have to live in a wet muddy cold pig pen. What makes the difference?" Well, the cow pondered for a moment, as cows are wont to do, and finally she said, "Well, I don't know. But maybe it's because I give a return to the farmer every day from what he gives me. He has to wait for you to die before he gets yours."

Giving becomes a privilege because it is one way that I can make a return to God for all the things he has given me.

And, then, on the heels of that there is a second thing I'd like to suggest.

Giving is a privilege because it is through what I give that I am able to make myself into the kind of person I want to be.

It's always a surprise to me to recognize anew every year the subject that Jesus talked about most. It came to me once as a part of an experiment. A group of us were doing a Bible research project and were asked the question, what subject did Jesus talk about most? And we all guessed about it. And the guesses were what you might expect. Some guessed "the love of God." Others guessed "prayer" or "forgiveness." And then, with Bibles printed with the words of Jesus in red, we dug in and this is what we discovered. Fully one-sixth of all the verses in the New Testament had to do with a man and his possessions. One third of all Jesus' parables had to do with the right use of material things. The subject Jesus talked about most was the subject of a man and his money. And he did because in no other way can a person's character be seen as deeply or as quickly as in seeing where the person spends his money. Someone once put it this way. "If you want to know about a man's religion, don't ask him what he thinks about Jesus Christ. Ask him what he thinks about his property." And a writer of historical biography one time said the same thing when he said, "show me where a man spends his money and I will show you the real man." And Jesus himself put it best when in the sixth chapter of St. Matthew we read his words, "For where your treasure is, there shall your heart be also."

You see, what we do with our money, and especially that to which we will give our money, is a major measure of the kind of person we are.

Edwin Markham, the poet, tells a modern parable that illustrates the fact.

A certain rich man, it seems, wanted to do something good. One day he saw a hovel in which a poor carpenter lived with a large family. After some deep thought, the rich man went to see the carpenter and gave him plans for a beautiful new house. He asked the carpenter if he would build him such a house on a certain lovely spot on a hill on the edge of town.

"I want it to be as fine and as sturdy as possible," he said. "Use only the best materials and employ only the best workmen. Spare no expense to make it the finest house in town."

He said he was going on a journey and hoped the house would be ready when he returned. Well, the carpenter saw his chance. Other men with the same opportunity would make plenty for themselves on the side. Why shouldn't he? So he skimped on materials. He employed inexperienced and inexpensive help and covered their mistakes with paint.

So when the rich man returned, the house was finished. The carpenter brought the keys to him.

"I followed your instructions," he lied. "I have completed the house as you told me."

"I'm glad," the rich man said. "Here are the keys. They are yours. I had you build that house for yourself. You and your family are to live in it."

And that's the parable of life. We are building the houses we live in the rest of our lives. Our character, our habits, our interests, the things we enjoy, these are built day by day. And the way we spend our money, the things to which we will give our money, is, according to Jesus, a determining factor in how the house is to be finished. "For where your treasure is, there shall your heart be also."

And you see, that makes my giving, then, a real privilege. For by my giving, I am able to make myself into the kind of person I want to be.

Well, there they are. Two simple, but, I believe, very profound thoughts that I earnestly hope will be the foundation on which our stewardship will be considered.

Giving is a privilege because . . .

. . . it is one way I can return to God of what He has given me.

. . . it is a major way I can become the kind of person I want to be.

And maybe these are the things that Jesus had in mind when he said, "It is *more blessed* to give than to receive."

Exhibit 11

SERMON ON THE CHURCHES' MISSION
  (Example 2)

This morning we enter the second Sunday of our three week Every Member Canvass Program here at St. Stephen's. Next Sunday is a critical Sunday in the life of our parish because on that day, November 18, every family in our parish will be invited to make a financial commitment to God through this church. Pledging will be done in church, immediately following the sermon. Our pledges will then be offered to God on the Altar as part of our direct commitment to Him for 1974. And then, that afternoon, next Sunday, eighty Stewards will go out to call on our fellow church members who have not yet pledged. By that evening, November 18, with your cooperation, we hope to have about 85 percent to 90 percent of our program complete. Then we will be able to go to work joyfully on what we earnestly hope will be the expanded budget our financial pledges will allow us to create.

Last week, as we began this effort, we tried to say something about a view of life, that we believe, puts a foundation under our giving. We give, we tried to say, as a way of returning to God out of the many things He has given us. We give, we tried to say, because the things on which we spend our money, the things to which we are willing to give our money, is the most accurate measure of the kind of people we are, the kind of people we are in the process of becoming. And behind those two concepts, behind that philosophy of sharing, if you will, is our belief that fundamentally our giving is not to the church. We give to God. And the church is the vehicle through which our Christian giving to God can be channeled.

Now, this morning, with that as the foundation, we want to move to another concern in regard to our Stewardship. And that concern is the life of our parish, the life of St. Stephen's Church.

One of the serious questions, sometimes one of the nightmares, with which a parish rector and vestry has to live is the question, "Are we really doing what we ought to be doing as a parish?" Someone once said that a parish rector needs to have what is termed "a creative uneasiness" about his parish. And out of that uneasiness, the questions seem to come rather often. "What are we doing here as a parish?" "What are we really accomplishing?" and "What are we not doing that we ought to do, or ought to do better?"

Well, this morning, to speak to those questions in some fashion, I'd like to tell you a story. It's a story about a parish church and what it is and maybe even about what it could be. Maybe it's a story about St. Stephen's. And it begins in Devil's Lake, North Dakota or in Northbrook, Illinois, or in Saratoga, California, or wherever you want it to.

The man's name is Bob, Robert C. Long, III, to be exact, but Bob to everyone who knew him. It had really come as no surprise. In fact, he had rather been hoping for it. It would be their third move in the past nine years. But maybe this would be the last one. A family had to sink it's roots somewhere, and maybe suburban Minneapolis might just be the right place. The move was hurried and hectic, as all their moves had been, but they weathered it very well.

And their new home was very nice. Just new enough to be modern but not so new as not to have some real charm about it. Bob had made friends through his work and

Marge, his wife, had met some people in the neighborhood and through the school. And everyone seemed pretty happy about it.

And now, three years later, as Bob thought back on it, he mused, "Yes, it really had happened very easily."

But it wasn't the move that occupied Bob's thoughts on this day as much as it was the church they had decided to go to. The Church had always been important to Bob and his family. In all their moves, it was the Church that had been one of their rocks of stability. And in the new place they had found a church that had some appeal for them and they had joined and pitched right in.

"It's funny," he mused, "how churches, almost like people, have a feel about them, a character all their own." And he remembered the first time he had ever come to this place. His first impression was from the building. It was a beautiful thing, L-shaped, sitting on a corner with vines growing up the sides. And on the inside it was just what he expected a church should look like. High gothic arches and soft light and a magnificent Altar. "The people who built this place really knew something about building churches," he thought. And then, because Bob was an engineer, his mind took a strange turn. He's seen the corner-stone that set the time of building at 1939. And he began to think, "I wonder if they are having any problems with it. A building like this, in 35 years is going to have some problems with roofs and stone work and the heating plant and motors and controls." But he supposed, that there were no such problems here. It looked so clean and neat. It wasn't until much later that, as a visitor to a Vestry meeting, he discovered that indeed there were some problems, many of them, with which the Vestry was wrestling, major problems of repair and replacement. And being an engineer he knew there was always going to be something needed. That was one of the reasons he had raised his pledge last year.

But that was much later. And now, his mind was back on that first Sunday and he remembered that his reverie about the building was sharply broken by the clatter of what seemed a hundred feet clapping up the stairs. It was the junior choir getting ready for worship and that was not the only sound. In fact, the whole narthex was a noisy place. Bob had heard noise in churches before, the noise of dissension and quarreling but that wasn't the sound at all. It was a much happier sound. The sound of friendship and greeting. And, indeed, his instinct about the noise proved out, as after Church, several parish members had spoken to him and to his wife and greeted them as visitors. That impressed Bob almost as much as anything on that first day. And, then, there was another sound, too. It was a sound that was hard to describe because sometimes it was no sound at all. It took him several weeks to really pin it down.

But later he began to know it as the sound of worship. It was the sound of people singing and praying and listening and doing all these things together, a beautiful sound, a sound that had a deepening note of sincerity about it. And you know when he identified it? One Sunday when he didn't hear it. One Sunday, when for some reason he couldn't fathom, the service was flat and dull. Maybe it was his own state of mind that made it seem that way. But that day made him realize just how much the strong sound of responsiveness and genuiness in worship could mean and how very often he had heard it in this place.

Well, noise got him to thinking about children. And children got him thinking about education. And that was something else he had learned about this church. It was commited to a continually improving program of Christian education. And it began with adults. There were Bible studies in the mornings, and classes in the evenings and

Prayer Groups. And he understood there was to be a major adult Bible study program launched in 1974 called the Bethel Bible Series. Eventually it was to involve almost half the adults in the parish. And there seemed to be a fairly steady stream of adult seminars offered to help people learn and live as Christians. And he remembered something someone had once said about the church. "The church works best when its like a maternity ward, where ideas are continually being given birth and re-birth in people's minds and where new life is continually nurtured and starts to grow." And he guessed maybe that this parish was a little like that.

That thought made him shift his gears to start thinking about Sunday School. It was almost a shift from the sublime to the ridiculous. It wasn't really that at all. But the first Sunday, three years ago, had made him smile. There were kids all over the place—kids of every size and shape, noisy kids, well-behaved kids, serious kids and kids who had just a little touch of devilment in them. "I'll bet some of those are a real handful in class," he thought. But then what more important thing can you do than to teach children. Later he found some words in a trade magazine that seemed to describe how he felt about teaching children in church. They were written by Daniel Webster. He had clipped it out and given a copy to the rector.

> "If we work on marble, it will perish.
> If we work on brass, time will efface it.
> If we rear temples, they will crumble to dust.
> But if we work on children's immortal minds,
> if we imbue them with high principles,
> with the just fear of God and love of
>   their fellow men,

we engrave on those tables something
that no time can efface,
And which will brighten and brighten
unto eternity."

Well, maybe Webster's poetry didn't exactly match what went on in some Sunday School classes on a given Sunday, but over the long haul that's what it was all about, "engraving ideas and principles on children's minds." It occurred to him to wonder how all that was paid for, the materials and machines and training and planning and coordination of it all. But as soon as he wondered, he knew. It was his pledge and that of many, many others that got the job done. And he was glad to add some extra to his pledge every year to see that that got done well.

Well, it was several weeks later that he got another impression about this parish. It's funny how it happened. He had driven by the church one night about 9:30 and the place was ablaze with light. As far as he knew, there was no parish program that night and it intrigued him enough to ask someone what was going on. Well, it turned out to be a community group that was using the building. In fact, he learned that there were ten separate groups from the community using the church building every single week. Three Alcoholics Anonymous groups, two Girl Scout Troops, a Boy Scout Troop, a Bluebird Pack, the Cerebral Palsy Association, the Lion's Club and one group called Emotions Anonymous. For a total of 18–20 hours every single week, the church building was open for the use of the community. Now that's community service, he thought. Not the kind that finds its way into the newspaper very often, but important community service nonetheless! And it somehow made him feel good about his parish even though it probably cost them something for light and heat and wear and tear and such like.

And that's when he began to get his first negative thoughts about the parish. Because he began to think about community service. It's all well and good to have these groups in the building. And he understood that many of the seminars drew people from outside the parish and that's community service, too. And he had checked and discovered that it was parish policy to give away 21 percent of all budget income to programs outside the parish, to the Diocese primarily. And the more he knew about the people of the parish, the more he discovered that, individually, there were a great many of them giving all kinds of time and skills to outside service programs, perhaps, he thought, because they had been motivated to do so, in part, by the Gospel being preached in this church. But he couldn't help wondering if there might not be something missing, something the church was not doing, something he really wished they could do. Maybe it was old-fashioned but what would happen if his parish were to consider adopting a mission somewhere. Maybe in Africa or in South America or the Philippines or New Guinea, or Appalachia or South Dakota. What if there was a church or Christian medical mission or a Christian school somewhere that was really touching people's minds and bodies in the name of Jesus Christ. Surely, there were a multitude of such things, desperately looking for the kind of help we could give. Such a thing could add a whole new dimension of life to the parish. If indeed, the Rector had been right, that we become the kind of people we are by the things to which we are willing to give our money, then maybe that was true of the parish as a whole as well. It seemed like such a good idea to him. And he wondered if it was just a matter of having enough money to go ahead and do it. His mind almost raced away from him as he began to consider the possibilities. And he knew that he would be willing to put a lot of thought and time into it, if the parish would accept the idea and be willing to support it.

What was it Jesus had said? "I come not to be ministered unto but to minister." Yes, that was it. And somehow he knew that every parish worth the name Christian had to see itself in that way, as an agent of ministry to those outside itself. Well, he'd be sure to speak to the Rector about it. And, if there was enough money pledged in 1974, maybe it could be brought to pass here in this place. And he began to wonder how many things there were that simply can't be dreamed about because there isn't enough money to convert dreams into reality.

And as he thought about that, suddenly his reverie was broken as his wife came down from upstairs. "Gee, we'd better hurry," she said. "It's already a quarter to nine. The church service begins in fifteen minutes. I understand the Rector is going to be talking today about the parish, for the Every Member Canvass. I wonder what he is going to say."

Exhibit 12

Some years ago, an English preacher went into his pulpit
to deliver his sermon. While he was announcing his text, he
saw a member of his congregation settling down comfort-
ably for a short nap. The good preacher noticing the man
said to his congregation, "If anyone can fall asleep while I
am preaching, he is fully entitled to do so; the blame is
mine. But a friend here today is taking unfair advantage of
me. He's going to sleep before I even begin. That's not fair.
At least, we have to start even."

Today is Pledge Sunday here at St. Stephen's. And what I
have to say to you will have to do with your pledge and
mine to God. Now I don't know how you feel about the
so-called money sermon and paying close attention to it. But
I'd like to make that bargain with you now. At least, let's
start even.

For the past two weeks we have tried to lay some
foundations under our considerations of giving to God. We
have said that your giving and mine needs to be thought of
in terms of our return to God for what God has abundantly
given to us. We have said that what we are as persons is
determined, in large measure, by the things to which we are
willing to give our money. And last week, through a story,
we tried to suggest some of the things to which we are
committed here as a parish, things that cost us money; a
large, complex building needing constant work, an expand-

ing education program for both children and adults. Giving of 21 percent of our pledge income outside of our parish, and a missionary thrust still in the dream stage but hopeful of achievement as soon as we can. And to these things we could easily have added our Youth Program needs, our music needs and the need to maintain proper salaries and benefits for the six full-time and four part-time people who work for us here. All these things are before us in some expanded form for 1974.

The foundation laid on those two Sundays has now brought us to the day on which each of us must make our decision about our pledge to God through this church. And the question before us is the question of knowing where to draw the line. When that moment comes to sign the card, how are you and how am I going to draw the line?

There are a number of ways in which you can make your decision, in which you can draw the line. And I'd like briefly to suggest just three of them for your honest thought and prayer.

To begin with, it is possible for you to draw the line in a minimal fashion.

One time, Jesus was starting out on a trip and a man came to Him and asked, "Good Teacher, what must I do to get to heaven?"

"Well," Jesus replied, "you know the Commandments."

"Yes, I do. In fact, I haven't broken a single one since I was very young."

"You lack only one thing, then." Jesus said, "Go and sell all you have and give to the poor and come and follow me."

And then we read, "The man's face fell and he went away, for he was very rich."

I've always felt that that's one of the saddest stories in the New Testament. And, for me anyway, its sadness stems from the fact that the man who came to Jesus was a good man, a man of character, a man really dedicated to high moral standards in the Commandments. But he was a man who was never quite able to make the connection between his morality and his money. And Jesus knew that. That's why He challenged him the way He did. When it came to his money, his morality collapsed. He drew the line in a minimal fashion and he missed out on being one of the first disciples of Jesus.

I guess, to be realistic, we do have to say that there are those in the church today who draw the line in the same way. Now, to be sure, God doesn't come to us and ask us to sell all we have and give to the poor. But he does ask us to return to Him a responsible portion of what we have. And to that request, there are those who do let their faces fall and walk away.

It was Voltaire who was credited with the remark that "When it comes to money, everyone is of the same religion." Money is the one God, according to Voltaire, that is universally worshipped. Now, we know that he was far too cynical about people to be right about that. But you and I also know the kind of people that he was thinking about. There are people whose money goes in quantity to everything they think they want or need, everything except the things that matter most. They are the people who are a little like the map a salesman found one time in a hotel room. It marked all the principal places of interest in the city and how to get to them from the hotel. It showed the theaters, the night clubs, the ball park, the best restaurants, the department stores, the post office, and the police station. But on the map there wasn't a single church marked anywhere. The advertisement said that the hotel was at the heart of the city, nearest to everything important. But it left out the most important thing of all.

There are those who may want to draw the line this

morning in that fashion. All these things and a minimum for God in the church.

But there is another way that some will draw the line. You can draw the line in an impulsive fashion.

Just before the Passover Festival, Jesus was in the house of a man named Simon, the leper. During the supper, a woman came in and, taking a flask of very expensive perfume, broke the seal and poured it over Jesus' head as a gift of adoration. Immediately, those around her complained at her impulsive waste. "Why, she could have sold that perfume and given the money to the poor." But Jesus accepted the gift saying, "Let her alone; why berate her for doing a good thing."

To Jesus, the woman's adoration was a very generous act, one that He was most willing to accept. But it was a very impulsive one as well, a once in a lifetime kind of giving.

Recently, this fall, as the Chairman of our Diocesan Department of Stewardship, I attended a meeting of our Diocesan Council. I found myself trying very hard to raise their thinking sights away from the nitty-gritty of a very tight diocesan budget in which they were necessarily engrossed. And, in the middle of this, I said to them, "What would you do if someone, at this moment, walked in that very door and gave us a check for a million dollars? What would you do with it?" Instantly four or five people spoke out and said, "We'd pass a quick motion to accept it."

And, of course, we too, like Jesus would accept that kind of impulsive gift here at St. Stephen's. Let me assure you if anyone in this congregation is moved to give this morning in an impulsive and bountiful way, I say to you, "Blessings on you."

But perhaps you would permit me to say that, for most of us, that kind of impulsive giving tends to be occasional, spasmodic, ill-proportioned, very generous today and very cautious tomorrow. And, quite honestly, for most of us, not for all, but for most of us, that kind of giving tends to be easier to put on a pledge card today than it is to pay in full later on.

There indeed may be some of you this morning that are called to make that kind of impulsive gift. But for most of us, giving needs to be thoughtful, methodical, systematic and not dependent on our feelings of the moment.

One of the great and wealthy American statesmen of this generation some years ago wrote to his son about giving. He said, "In regard to money as well as time, there is a great advantage in its methodical use. Especially is it wise to dedicate a certain portion of our means to purposes of charity and religion. The great advantage of having a definite portion set aside is that when we are asked to give, the competition is never between self on the one hand and charity on the other, but between the different purposes of religion and charity, among which we can then make the most careful choice."

To be sure, warmly and thankfully, Jesus accepted the impulsive gift. He even called it "a good thing." But He also called men to a thoughtful, measured, conscientious kind of sharing.

And that brings us to the third way you can draw the line. You can draw the line with a conscientiously measured, responsible return to God out of what God has given you.

One of the most thought provoking parables Jesus ever told was the parable of the talents. "A householder," Jesus said, "gave certain gifts to each of three men. To one he gave ten talents, to another five, and to another, one talent." And he said to them, "trade with these until I return." The ten talent man returned ten talents more. The five talent man returned five talents more. But the one talent man, fearful that he would lose the one talent he had, hoarded it and returned nothing. To the first two, the householder said, "Well done thou good and faithful servant." But to the third, he said, "Thou wicked and slothful servant . . . take the talent from him . . . and cast the worthless servant into the darkness."

And the point of the parable is not that people have varying amounts given to them but that every person, regardless of the size of what he has, is expected to make some return in proportion to what he does have.

You know, the easiest thing in the world to do, and something I am tempted to do every year at this time, is to stand up here and tell you about our budget needs for the next year. We could dramatize those needs very easily, I'm sure. Some of you may have wondered why we haven't talked more about those things. But every year, we are able to resist that temptation. Because to do so would be to ask you to support a program here in this church. And much as we need that support, it is my deep, deep conviction that we are not called to be program supporters, but we are called to be Christian stewards. We are not called to support a budget but we are called, in thanksgiving, to make a conscientious return to God out of what we have. Maybe the difference I'm trying to suggest, and, in this context what the parable of the talents is trying to suggest is this. To give out of what we own to support a budget is called philanthropy. To give as a thankful return to God out of what we have is called Christian Stewardship. And I believe the Lord is calling us to be Christian stewards.

And how can any one of us do that? It's really very simple. All you need do is take your income, that most concrete measure of what you do have, and apply to that income whatever proportion you feel is the conscientious, responsible percentage you wish to return to God through this church. Many Christians, a significant number in this parish, have become modern tithers, that is, they make a pledge of 5 percent of their income to God through the Church. That leaves the other 5 percent of the tithe for giving outside the Church. A larger number in this parish, unable to jump to 5 percent all at once, began last year pledging 3 percent of their income to God. Some, in this parish are already full tithers, pledging 10 percent of income. But wherever you feel you can begin, the important thing is that you and I do begin seeing our pledge as a responsible portion of income returned to God. You can draw the line with a conscientiously measured, responsible return to God out of what God has given you.

And perhaps the conclusion of the matter for this whole parish is a little story.

A doctor in a French village was about to retire. For years he had been on call day and night, caring for people's illnesses. And often without payment. As the day of his retirement approached, the village wished to do something for him. Because people had so little money, it was decided that as a concrete expression of their gratitude and affection, each family would bring a pitcher of wine from their own cellar and pour it into a large barrel placed in the village square. Well, the day arrived and all day long villagers were seen pouring their offerings into the barrel. The evening came and the barrel was taken to the doctor's home and presented to him with great expressions of warmth. And when it was done, the doctor, somewhat overwhelmed by all this, went to the barrel, dipped into it and drank the first of this great gift. The drink was a shock. It tasted like water. He dipped again. And again it was water. Surely there must have been some queer mistake. But no, the barrel was filled with water. And then, the truth was exposed. Everyone in the town had reasoned, "That's a big barrel. My little pitcher of wine won't be missed. I have so little for myself. This is a big village. The others will take care of it." And an expression of gratitude became an expression of tragedy.

This is a big parish.

You can draw the line in a minimal fashion.

You can draw the line in an impulsive fashion.

You can draw the line in a conscientious fashion.

How you and I draw the line is now a matter between you, your family, and your God.

Let us pray.

Almighty God, whose loving hand has given us all that we possess: Grant us grace that we may honor you with our substance. Help us to see that we are unworthy of your blessings, unless we share them with others. Bless our effort in this Every Member Canvass, and remembering the account we must one day give, help us as people and parish to be faithful stewards of your bounty through Jesus Christ Our Lord. AMEN.

By Oscar C. Carr, Jr.

"MONEY IS NOT A FOUR-LETTER WORD"

The author, The Rev. John MacNaughton, and I first met in June 1974 at a provincial conference on Stewardship Motivation and Development in Denver, Colorado, where he made the principal address. The evaluation sheets from the participants in that conference described Father MacNaughton's comments as "Inspiring—Stimulating —Refreshing—Thought Provoking—Practical—Effective." When I expressed my hope that these remarks could be shared with a wider fellowship, Father MacNaughton said he did have a manuscript entitled, "Money Is Not a Four-Letter Word." Agreeing that the book was a good idea—the title superb—the connection was made with The Seabury Press and "Stewardship: Myth and Methods" is the happy result.

Reliable sources inform me that it is the prerogative of a book publisher to change an author's suggested title. I not only respect that prerogative, but the extraordinary talents of Werner Mark Linz, President of The Seabury Press, as well. On the matter of *this* book, however, we did not agree—and I am absolutely delighted that he asked me to write this afterword.

Some theologians argue with the premise that giving money leads to conversion or commitment, believing that stewardship results from conversion. Father MacNaughton reminds us that Jesus put it the other way around. "Where your *treasure is,* there will your heart be *also!*" (Matthew 6:21)

When we give money to God through his church, we are giving part of ourselves. We are sharing our love, our concern, our friendship, our personhood. The giving is a conscious act of the brain we have been given to think with, the gift an output of the body we have been given to work with, a reflection of the raw materials of this world we have been given to create with—all in proportion to the opportunities we have been given with which to grow and learn and mature and develop as people. Stewardship really involves our very life—all that we do, all the time—and is an expression in thanksgiving for that life. To paraphrase, "the measurement of thanksgiving through sharing," is to suggest that "money is not a four-letter word."

This is a message the church needs to hear and heed. Not only does this book set the biblical and theological basis for this approach to stewardship, but the author describes in detail the methods by which the parish leadership can challenge the congregation, consistent with this biblical theology of money.

The Office of Development of the Episcopal Church has no higher priority than to increase the level of giving by improved church-wide stewardship. We are building a network of professional consultants—such as Father Mac-Naughton—who are eager to assist those who desire help. We are accumulating resource materials such as this book. We trust there will be more to come.

The late Thomas Frank Gailor, the third Episcopal Bishop of the Diocese of Tennessee, told a delightful story when he went on fund-raising trips for the University of the South at Sewanee. He said that a man once received a note signed, "The Black Hand." It read, "Put $5,000 in the hollow stump in the cemetry at the stroke of midnight or we will kidnap your wife." At the appointed hour, the extortioners arrived at the stump to find not the $5,000, but a polite reply which read, "I am very sorry that I do not have $5,000, but I want you to know how very much I favor your movement!"

Too many of us—for much too long—have been just "in favor of the stewardship movement." This book gives us a method that cuts through such rhetoric and myth. While the author would be the first to agree that his book does not suggest the *only* method for effective stewardship, it is a way—a tested way—that has been successful. We heartily commend it, not only to your attention, but for your continued use.

One final word about stewardship. There comes a point in the life of every individual—as in the momentum of every institution—when one "votes" either to go forward or to turn back. To stand still or stay dormant—to maintain the status quo—is to begin to die—to in effect, turn back by *not* moving forward. The vote takes place in the mind—in the collective attitude, at the commitment level—not in any public polling place. The outcome is nonetheless decisive. Those of us who care about the human community, as we express these Christian concerns through the Episcopal Church, are casting our votes *now*. Our response to the inspirations and demands of the Gospel we profess to believe can be measured by the manner in which we address ourselves to the ministry and mission opportunities that abound. As we continue this lifelong process—this quest—and that's what it really is—we recognize there is ample room for growth in each of us. Since stewardship, really, is learning how to live, the rewards can be immense.

The very best of luck in *your* quest.

And don't forget "money is *not* a four-letter word!"

Oscar C. Carr, Jr.
Executive for Development/Stewardship
The Episcopal Church
New York City
1 March 1975

81